Everybody Loves Meatloaf

Also by Melanie Barnard

Low-Fat Grilling

The Best Covered and Kettle Grill Cookbook Ever

365 *More* Ways to Cook Chicken

Marinades

With Brooke Dojny

Parties!

Cheap Eats

Sunday Suppers

Let's Eat In

Everybody Loves

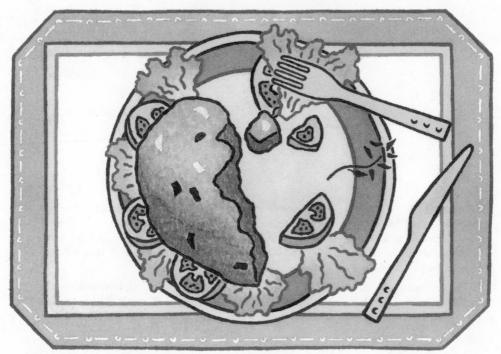

Meatloaf

MORE THAN
100 RECIPES FOR LOAVES AND FIXIN'S

Melanie Barnard

HarperPerennial
A Division of HarperCollinsPublishers

HarperCollins books may be purchased for educational, business, or sales promotional use. For information please write: Special Markets Department, HarperCollins Publishers, Inc., 10 East 53rd Street, New York, NY 10022.

FIRST EDITION

Design by Stephanie Tevonian

Illustrations by Melanie Marder Parks

Library of Congress Cataloging-in-Publication Data

Barnard, Melanie.
    Everybody loves meatloat : more than 100 recipes for loaves and fixin's /
by Melanie Barnard. — 1st ed.
        p.   cm.
    Includes index.
    ISBN 0-06-095219-9
    I. TITLE.
TX749.B37   1997
641.8'24—dc21   97-4134

97 98 99 00 01 ❖/RRD 10 9 8 7 6 5 4 3 2 1

This book is dedicated to the memory of my maternal grandmother, Cecilia Shepard Gillis, who gave me meatloaf and more

Contents

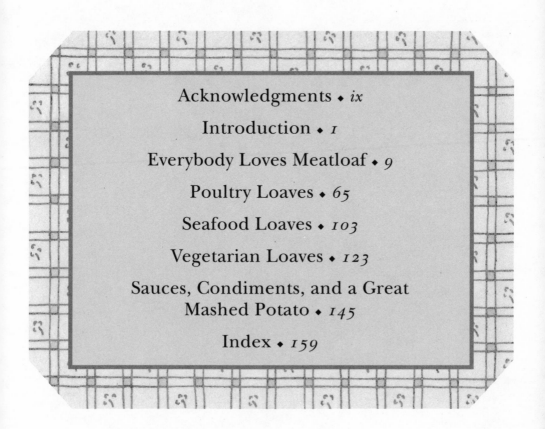

Acknowledgments

*M*ore than any other book I've written, this one garnered opinions and ideas, recipes and clippings from friends and family alike.

I asked my mother for a couple of her favorites, and she, true to form, produced dozens of recipes—all carefully handwritten, clipped together, and with advice on how to change and improve each and every one—and a final note that she was very proud of me. (She is Grandma's daughter, after all.)

I asked my husband and grown sons for their input. They, having previously existed for long periods of time on chicken and barbecue as I worked on other books, did smilingly reassure me that they would love each and every meatloaf they were about to taste. These are men of character and good appetite.

I asked my friend and writing partner, Brooke Dojny, if I could use a couple of her recipes, and she gave me full access to every meatloaf recipe she had ever written. This unconditional generosity defines Brooke.

I sought guidance from my longtime editor, Susan Friedland, and she characteristically gave little other than a few basic directions and a comment that she had complete faith in the work that I would produce. This kind of free rein on a firm rope is what makes Susan a truly great editor.

I asked for advice from my agent, Judith Weber, and she said a meatloaf book is incomplete without a good mashed potato recipe. This kind of seeing beyond the forest and into the trees is why Judith is so well respected in the food-writing community.

Thanks to each and every one of you.

Introduction

My maternal grandmother, Cecilia Shepard Gillis, made a very fine meatloaf. In fact, she made many good meatloaves, and took great pride in the preparation and serving of each one. Meatloaf-making was my first home-cooking lesson. Grandma taught me to mix gently, to pat smoothly, and to tend the loaf carefully during baking. Over forty years later, as I write this book, I realize that she was talking about a lot more than meatloaf.

The modern meatloaf, like other widely loved foods such as pizzas, pastas, and burgers, has expanded its horizons well beyond the traditional definition. The new meatloaf may be chicken or turkey, salmon or shrimp, or may not even have any meat in it at all! This book is a celebration of all meatloaves, old and new, meat or not.

After years of being held in high esteem in the American food world, meatloaf fell into disfavor during the last decade. It became the butt of school cafeteria jokes, and it was the centerfold of gluey gravy-stained diner menus. Meatloaf was relegated to the kitchen closet, and rarely discussed in polite culinary company.

It is good news indeed that meatloaf has lately made a comeback! And why not? It has all the right stuff for the way we cook today—easy to make and serve, very versatile, economical, nutritionally correct, usually good hot or cold, and loved by practically everyone.

Depending upon the occasion, meatloaf can be a culinary masterpiece, or it can be a flavorful everyday menu staple. In my view, it is both. There are loaves for celebrations—say, a rich pâtélike loaf with some mellow red wine. And then there are loaves to brighten the most mundane of days—hearty slices of ground meats bound together with good bread crumbs and topped with ketchup and bacon.

In researching this book, I found that nearly everyone has a meatloaf story, ranging from a gravy incident with a sibling to a romance over a little shrimp mousse and champagne on New Year's Eve. In addition, nearly everyone I know has a meatloaf recipe, but very few have more than one. So, because we can never get enough of a good thing, here are a few more meatloaves to add to your collection, as well as a repertoire of poultry, seafood, and vegetarian loaves, all designed to give you a whole new view on this American classic.

The Ingredients

If you want good vegetables, you have to plant good seeds.
  ✦ Grandma Gillis

*L*oaves, whether meat, poultry, seafood, or vegetable, all consist of four categories of ingredients: a main protein, a starch, a binder, and seasonings. Whatever type of loaf, a worthy finished product is a mix of the highest-quality ingredients.

The Main Protein: For most of the loaves in this book, about 1½ pounds of uncooked meat, poultry, seafood, or vegetables are geared to serve six people. This fits nicely into recommended nutritional guidelines, and also fits nicely into the average loaf pan.

The Basic Meatloaf Mix: Extremely tasty and interesting meatloaves can be made entirely from a single type of meat, and many of my loaves are. But I've also found that a basic meatloaf mix of about *¾ pound lean ground beef chuck and about 6 ounces each of lean ground pork and veal makes a wonderful loaf.* It doesn't really matter if the proportions are off by a bit. Many supermarkets sell this combination (usually about equal parts of each meat), and you can certainly request such a mix from the butcher.

Whatever meat or combination you use, be sure that it is lean and well trimmed of all visible fat before grinding, but don't waste your time or money on cuts that are ultraexpensive, such as ground Porterhouse steak, or extra-lean, such as pork tenderloin. They are likely to produce a dry, less flavorful result. For the juiciest loaf, use only fresh, not previously frozen meat.

The Basic Poultry Loaf: Most poultry loaves feature either ground turkey or chicken, both of which are widely available these days. In most cases, they are interchangeable within recipes, but be aware that ground chicken is somewhat softer than ground turkey, so you may need to add a bit more binder to give substance to the finished loaf. Commercially ground poultry varies widely in its composition; some is ground from skinless breast meat only (the most expensive) while others contain many parts, including skin. You may use whatever you like, but I prefer a pure blend of skinless white and dark meat—ask your butcher or read the label for the exact ingredients in your package. Whatever you use, be sure it is fresh and has not been frozen or it may produce a watery loaf.

The Basic Seafood Loaf: Good loaves can be made from a single type of seafood, especially if it is assertively flavored, such as salmon. But many delicate seafoods, such as sole or shrimp benefit from working in combination to produce the best texture and flavor. Because the seafood is to be ground up anyway, this is a good time to buy odd cuts, such as the end cuts of salmon or smaller shrimp, all of which are likely to be far less expensive than perfect steaks or jumbo shrimp. Do not, however, scrimp on freshness.

The Basic Vegetarian Loaf: Most vegetarian loaves are based on grains and/or legumes because they provide texture and substance to the loaf. Whether you cook your own, from fresh or dried, or open a can, start with good-quality ingredients for the best flavor.

The Starch: The starch is what gives the characteristic juicy and slightly soft texture to a loaf, acting as a sponge to absorb and retain the flavorful juices. The starch can be fresh or dried bread crumbs, cracker crumbs, cereal, rice, or even pasta. My choice for most loaves is fresh bread crumbs made from the best-quality firm bread, though in some loaves dry bread crumbs, or rice in conjunction with bread crumbs, give an interesting texture. For a loaf with 1½ pounds of main protein, approximately 1 cup of fresh crumbs is about right.

Sometimes the bread crumbs contribute their own flavor, such as recipes calling for rye or whole wheat bread, but in most cases the role of the starch is to carry flavor and moisture, and thus white bread crumbs are most often called for. I like the bread to be firm and slightly dry. Crumbs are a great way to use up day-old bread (especially the end pieces with all that flavorful crust), though really stale bread is better tossed to the birds than into a mixing bowl.

The Binder: A loaf is held together and moistened by the binder, and eggs do this job best. In most loaves, 2 eggs are my choice for 1½ pounds of the main protein or vegetable base, but if other protein-based liquids are used, especially dairy products like milk or yogurt, 1 egg will do the job. Like the starch, the binder is usually a bland flavor-carrying agent. If you are concerned about cholesterol, 2 egg whites or ¼ cup of cholesterol-free egg substitute can be used instead for each egg in a recipe.

The Seasonings: If the main protein, starch, and binder are the basic structure for good texture, then it is the job of the seasonings to turn a mundane mixture into a memorable meal. So begin with the best quality and add with an assertive hand.

Most loaves contain chopped onions and many contain garlic, carrots, celery, or other basic aromatic vegetables. In a few cases, these are added raw for their crunchy texture, but most recipes here call for a brief cooking of the vegetables to soften the texture and bring out the fullest flavor. In addition, cooked vegetables also contribute flavorful moisture that is absorbed by the bland starches and binders.

Spices turn up in many loaves and can be added directly to the mixing bowl, but sometimes a spice develops a more complex flavor if first heated before being stirred into the cooked aromatic vegetables. Spices do not have an infinite shelf life. Even with proper storage in a cool, dry, dark cupboard, they will lose potency over time and should be replaced at least once a year.

Herbs can be dried or fresh, and in most recipes I've given the option. Though I prefer the clean flavor of fresh herbs, good-quality dried herbs are better than limp, over-the-hill fresh herbs. However, a few herbs such as dill, basil, and parsley do not dry well and are only worthwhile fresh. Fortunately, these are also widely available fresh in supermarkets.

Commercial condiments from soy sauce to ketchup are wonderful seasonings, whether added directly to the mixing bowl or as part of a flavorful glaze. Again, quality going into the loaf means quality coming out of the oven.

Citrus juice and grated peel also contribute big flavor to loaves. Always use fresh juice and grate only the colored portion of the peel, leaving behind the bitter white pith.

The Mixing

Be swift and gentle.

   (Grandma again)

Use a generously sized mixing bowl; a 3-quart bowl is about right for most of these recipes. The ample space will allow you to mix with fewer strokes.

Use your hands to mix the ingredients together. I tried mixing ingredients with a fork, a mixing spoon, and even experimented with an electric mixer and a food processor. None works as well as a pair of clean hands. Just put the prepared ingredients in the bowl, then scoop up from the bottom and mix through open fingers to keep the ingredients as light and aerated as possible. This is not bread dough; don't knead or slap it around. Treat the loaf with care and mix just until everything is blended.

Pat into the pan or form and smooth into loaves with as much gentleness as you used in the mixing.

The Baking

A watched pot eventually boils.
What's the hurry?

   (Grandma had quite a bit to say)

Many meatloaf connoisseurs feel that the "crust" is the best part of the loaf. I agree. Most meatloaf and many poultry loaf recipes that are designed to be baked in a 9 by 5-inch loaf pan can also be shaped into a 9 by 5-inch loaf in a 13 by 9-inch baking pan. With more surface exposure to the heat of the oven, more crust will be formed. A bit of juiciness and moisture is lost in the process, but I think the crusty result is worth it. I've given the free-form and the pan option in recipes that can be baked either way.

If you want a really juicy result or like the presentation of a perfectly formed loaf, then the traditional loaf pan is the best choice. I've used both metal and glass loaf pans and metal or glass baking dishes. I like metal better (though glass works fine) since it seems to promote more browning and hence more "crust." There are also pans on the market now that are shaped like a standard loaf pan, but have a perforated bottom insert. The loaf is patted into the insert, which is then placed in the pan. The excess juices and fat drip through the perforations, which is said to give a lower-fat loaf. It also gives a somewhat drier loaf, but is an option for people for whom this is a real issue.

The loaf must be baked through completely, especially important since the ingredients include ground meat, poultry, or seafood, and eggs. Most loaves in a 9 by 5-inch pan bake in about 1 hour, and most in a 2-quart baking pan are cooked through in 45 to 50 minutes. To be sure, and because temperatures vary in even the best of ovens, an instant reading thermometer inserted into the center of the loaf will provide an accurate gauge. Meat and seafood should be cooked to 155 degrees, while poultry should reach 160 degrees. Each recipe includes a "standing time" during which the loaf will reabsorb juices for easier slicing, and will continue to cook with residual heat to elevate the temperature another five degrees. So be sure to wait the standing time after removal from the oven.

The Eating
Call the rest of the family. Wash up. It's suppertime.

(We're coming, Gram)

It's important to let all loaves, except barbecued or skillet mini-loaves, stand a bit before slicing or cutting into squares. Like a roast, the loaves need the time to reabsorb the flavorful juices. You will also have much neater slices or squares.

Leftover loaves should be promptly refrigerated, and most make great leftovers. Wherever applicable, I have given suggestions for some at the end of the recipe.

At our house, meatloaf etiquette requires that the adults be offered the end pieces, which are considered more desirable since they

Everybody Loves Meatloaf

have the most "crust." You may not find this in your manners book, but I still think that this kind of deference is a good thing to teach children. (Of course, about half the time, the adult smilingly defers to the youngster, especially if he or she had a hard day at school and needs a treat.)

Advanced Meatloaf

Once you have mastered Meatloaf 101, you will quickly move on to the advanced course. You will have the confidence and the sure hand to take the basic proportions and the mixing and baking instructions and personalize them with new and exciting combinations of ingredients. Meatloaf-making is a gift given to me by my grandmother, and I am honored to share it with you. Please pass it on.

Everybody Loves

Meatloaf

"Meat" Loaves

When I was young in BFF (Before Fast Food), truck stops were *the* places to stop and eat on long car trips. My grandparents, who were summer nomads and took me along on several of their adventures, rated truck stops according to the fullness of the parking lot. A ten-truck stop was a winner. I almost always ordered meatloaf, mostly because it came with gravy, mashed potatoes, and greens beans—other foods that were high on my favorite-food list in those ponytail and Elvis years. In my many truck-stop tastings, I learned that even the most basic meatloaf had hundreds of variations and that I could like them all because they were all recognizably meatloaf.

In the decades since then, I've come to love poultry, seafood, and vegetable loaves, but nothing quite replaces a "meat" loaf. So it is no coincidence that the largest chapter in this book is devoted to variations on true meatloaves.

Here you will find a couple of recipes for uncomplicated, classic all-American meatloaves, including a prizewinning loaf (prized by my family), some sophisticated international variations, such as Argentinian Steakloaf or Greek Lamb and Lentil Loaf, and a couple of deliciously wacky kid-loving ideas, such as The Big Meatball or a Bacon and Double Cheeseburger Loaf.

Many of the loaves call for specific amounts of a single meat or combination, but others call for "meatloaf mix," which is a blend of about one part each of lean ground pork and veal to two parts lean ground chuck. You can assemble this mix yourself or buy the "meatloaf mix" that is packaged in many supermarket meat departments. For most loaves, the ideal texture and taste is produced by this combination of sturdy, juicy beef along with tender and delicately flavored veal and pork.

Old-Fashioned Meatloaf

6 servings

*T*his is a slightly updated version of the meatloaf we had nearly once a week when I was a child. My mother often made it for Monday night supper, which luckily provided me with leftovers to pack for sandwiches in my Tuesday and Wednesday school lunch. Not only did I like this lunch a lot, it was eminently tradable, so sometimes I would pack two of them and barter one for a couple of those little packaged pink-frosted cakes that we never got at home. It is also the two parts lean ground beef chuck, one part ground pork, and one part ground veal mix that Mom used in this meatloaf that formed the basis for my own "meatloaf mix."

4 slices bacon

6 scallions

1 cup firm fresh white bread crumbs

2 tablespoons milk

2 tablespoons sour cream

1½ pounds "meatloaf mix" of ground chuck, pork, and veal

½ cup finely chopped onion

¼ cup finely chopped celery leaves

¼ cup chopped flat-leaf parsley

1½ tablespoons chopped fresh thyme or 1½ teaspoons dried

1 teaspoon salt

½ teaspoon freshly grated nutmeg

¼ teaspoon freshly ground pepper

2 cloves garlic, minced

2 eggs

½ cup bottled chili sauce

2 tablespoons light brown sugar

1 teaspoon dry mustard

Preheat the oven to 350 degrees. In a medium skillet over medium heat, cook the bacon until limp and some of the fat is rendered. Remove the bacon from the skillet and drain on paper towels. Thinly slice the scallions, separating white and green parts. In a small bowl, soak the bread crumbs in the milk and sour cream for 10 minutes.

In a large mixing bowl, use your hands to gently but thoroughly combine the meat, onion, celery leaves, parsley, thyme, salt, nutmeg, pepper, garlic, eggs, the sliced white part of the scallions, and the soaked bread crumbs and any liquid.

In a 13 by 9-inch baking pan, shape the meat into a 9 by 5-inch loaf or pat it into a 9 by 5-inch loaf pan, smoothing the top. Arrange bacon strips on top.

Everybody Loves Meatloaf

Bake for 35 minutes. Meanwhile, in a small bowl, combine the chili sauce, brown sugar, and mustard. Spread over the partially baked meatloaf. Sprinkle with the sliced scallion greens. Bake an additional 25 minutes or until the meatloaf is firm, the top is browned, and a meat thermometer inserted into the center of the loaf registers 155 degrees.

Let the meatloaf stand in the pan for 10 minutes before slicing to serve.

Leftovers: Make sandwiches with firm white sandwich bread, mayonnaise (my choice) or mustard (my sister's choice), thinly sliced tomato, and soft lettuce leaves.

Our Prizewinning Meatloaf

8 servings

*T*his recipe is reprised from *Sunday Suppers,* Brooke Dojny's and my first cookbook. At the time, it won the prize as the house favorite among our teenage children. Now that they are grown, they each have the recipe, and its easy preparation and great taste have made it part of their cooking repertoire—flattery that is much nicer for us than a prize any day.

2 pounds "meatloaf mix" of ground chuck, pork, and veal
1 cup milk
1 cup firm fresh white bread crumbs or uncooked quick oats
½ cup chopped flat-leaf parsley
⅓ cup finely chopped onion

1 egg
2 tablespoons prepared chili sauce or ketchup
1 tablespoon prepared horseradish
1¼ teaspoons salt
½ teaspoon freshly ground pepper

Preheat the oven to 375 degrees. In a large mixing bowl, use your hands to gently but thoroughly mix all of the ingredients.

In a 13 by 9-inch baking pan, shape the meat into a 9 by 5-inch loaf or pat it into a 9 by 5-inch loaf pan, smoothing the top. Bake about 1 hour until the meatloaf is firm, the top is richly browned, and a meat thermometer inserted into the center of the loaf registers 155 degrees.

Let the meatloaf stand in the pan for 10 minutes, then cut into slices to serve.

Leftovers: This is the loaf for a classic meatloaf sandwich on white bread with a little mustard or mayonnaise (or both) and some soft lettuce leaves.

Bacon and
Double Cheeseburger Loaf

6 servings

*T*love cheeseburgers, but I think that I like this meatloaf even better, especially when served with sesame-seed rolls and french fries. Unlike most meatloaf recipes, here the onion is mixed in raw so that it retains some crunchiness.

4 slices bacon
*1½ pounds lean ground chuck or
    ground round*
*1 cup firm fresh white
    bread crumbs*
*1 cup coarsely shredded sharp
    Cheddar cheese (about 4 ounces)*
*1 large sweet onion, such as
    Vidalia, chopped*

*2 tablespoons regular or low-fat
    mayonnaise*
*2 tablespoons India or other sweet
    pickle relish*
2 teaspoons dry mustard
¾ teaspoon salt
½ teaspoon freshly ground pepper
1 egg
¼ cup ketchup

Preheat the oven to 350 degrees. In a medium skillet, cook the bacon over medium heat until it is limp and some of the fat is rendered, 3 to 4 minutes. Remove the bacon from the skillet and reserve it.

In a large mixing bowl, use your hands to gently but thoroughly mix together the meat, bread crumbs, ½ cup of the cheese, onion, mayonnaise, relish, mustard, salt, pepper, and egg. Pat the mixture into a shallow 2-quart baking pan. Spread the top of the loaf with the ketchup, then lay the bacon strips over the ketchup. Bake until the loaf is firm and the bacon is crisp, 45 to 50 minutes, sprinkling the top of the loaf with the remaining ½ cup cheese to melt during the last 5 to 10 minutes of baking. Internal temperature should be 155 degrees. Let the meatloaf stand in the baking dish for 10 minutes, then cut into squares to serve.

Leftovers: Reheat slices in a microwave and serve on sesame buns with lettuce, tomato, and ketchup.

The Big Meatball

6 servings

*T*he extra-thick spaghetti, called perciatelli, is in scale with this meatball. Cut the meatball into wedges and serve on the spaghetti with the sauce. Or present it whole atop the pasta on a large platter.

1 pound lean ground chuck
½ pound hot or sweet Italian
*   sausage meat*
1 cup seasoned dry bread crumbs
½ cup chopped flat-leaf parsley
¼ cup grated Parmesan cheese
3 tablespoons chopped fresh basil or
*   2 teaspoons dried*

1 tablespoon chopped fresh oregano
*   or 1 teaspoon dried*
1 teaspoon salt
¼ teaspoon freshly ground
*   pepper*
3 eggs
4 cups homemade or bottled
*   marinara sauce*

Preheat the oven to 350 degrees. In a large mixing bowl, use your hands to gently but thoroughly combine the beef, sausage, bread crumbs, parsley, cheese, basil, oregano, salt, pepper, and eggs.

Place the meat in the center of a 13 by 9-inch baking dish. Use your hands to shape into a smooth rounded dome 3 to 4 inches high. Bake 35 minutes. Spoon or drain off any fat in the dish. Pour the marinara sauce over the loaf and bake 20 minutes more until a meat thermometer inserted into the center of the loaf registers 155 degrees. Let stand in the pan for 10 minutes.

Serve the meatloaf cut in wedges with about ⅔ cup sauce per serving.

Leftovers: Cut into chunks and reheat in additional marinara sauce. Serve spooned into hero or grinder rolls. Add a few slices of mozzarella cheese and some sautéed green peppers, if you wish.

Red Flannel Hash Loaf

6 servings

*H*ash is a close cousin to meatloaf, so this idea is a natural. You can even serve it for breakfast with poached eggs if you like.

*1 large waxy potato (about
   6 ounces), peeled and diced
   (about 1 cup)*
*1 small turnip (about 4 ounces),
   peeled and diced (about 1 cup)*
1 tablespoon vegetable oil
1 onion, chopped
1 carrot, chopped
*2 cups thinly sliced cabbage (about
   4 ounces)*
1½ pounds lean ground chuck

1 cup whole wheat bread crumbs
2 teaspoons Worcestershire sauce
1 teaspoon salt
½ teaspoon ground allspice
¼ teaspoon ground cloves
¼ teaspoon cayenne
1 egg
*4 small canned whole beets, diced
   (about 1 cup)*
3 tablespoons grainy Dijon mustard
1 tablespoon molasses

Cook the potato and turnip in boiling salted water to cover until tender, about 8 minutes. Drain. (The vegetables can be cooked a day ahead and refrigerated.)

Preheat the oven to 350 degrees. In a large skillet, heat the oil and cook the onion and carrot over medium heat, stirring often, for 3 minutes. Add the cabbage and cook, stirring often, until the vegetables are wilted, 3 to 4 minutes more.

In a large mixing bowl, use your hands to gently but thoroughly combine the meat, bread crumbs, Worcestershire, salt, allspice, cloves, cayenne, and egg. Add all of the cooked vegetables, including the beets, and mix into the meatloaf. Pat the mixture into a shallow 2-quart baking pan. In a small bowl, stir together the mustard and molasses. Brush over the top of the loaf.

Bake until the meatloaf is firm and the top is richly browned, 45 to 50 minutes.

Let the meatloaf stand in the dish for 5 to 10 minutes before cutting into squares to serve.

Swedish Meatloaf

6 servings

*A*s a mostly Italian child from a largely Italian community, I thought that the Swedish meatballs in dilled sour cream from the smorgasbord restaurant in our town were very exotic. I like the flavors even better now in meatloaf.

1 cup fresh rye bread crumbs
¼ cup milk
1 tablespoon vegetable oil
1 large onion, finely chopped
2 teaspoons all-purpose flour
¾ cup canned reduced-sodium beef broth
6 tablespoons chopped fresh dill

1½ pounds "meatloaf mix" of ground chuck, pork, and veal
1 tablespoon Dijon mustard
¾ teaspoon salt, plus additional to taste
½ teaspoon freshly ground pepper, plus additional to taste
½ teaspoon freshly grated nutmeg
½ cup sour cream or plain yogurt

Preheat the oven to 350 degrees. Soak the bread crumbs in the milk in a large mixing bowl for 10 minutes. In a large skillet, heat the oil and cook the onion over medium-low heat, stirring often until the onion is softened, about 5 minutes. Use a slotted spoon to transfer all but about 3 tablespoons of the onion to the bowl with the bread crumbs. Add the flour into the onion and drippings left in the skillet and cook, stirring over medium heat, for 1 minute. Whisk in the broth and 2 tablespoons of the dill and cook, stirring, until thickened and bubbly, about 2 minutes. Reserve the sauce.

Add the meat, mustard, ¾ teaspoon salt, ½ teaspoon pepper, nutmeg, and remaining 4 tablespoons of dill to the mixing bowl. Use your hands to gently but thoroughly mix together.

Pat the meatloaf into a shallow 2-quart baking pan. Bake until the meatloaf is firm and the top is well browned, 45 to 50 minutes. Let the meatloaf stand for 5 to 10 minutes in the pan while completing the sauce.

Reheat the sauce gently over medium-low heat until just bubbly. Remove from the heat and stir in the sour cream. Season with salt and pepper.

Cut meatloaf into squares and serve with the sauce spooned over.

Choucroute Loaf

6 servings

*I*n keeping with the flavors reminiscent of the Alsatian classic, serve this meatloaf with boiled potatoes and a salad of bitter greens with a cider vinaigrette.

¼ pound smoked ham
1 tablespoon vegetable oil
1 onion, chopped
1 tart apple, peeled, seeded, and
  coarsely chopped
2 cloves garlic, minced
1¼ pounds "meatloaf mix" of
  ground chuck, pork, and veal
1 cup rye bread crumbs

4 tablespoons prepared horseradish
1 tablespoon grainy Dijon mustard
1 tablespoon chopped fresh thyme
  or 1 teaspoon dried
1 teaspoon caraway seeds
½ teaspoon coarsely ground
  pepper
2 eggs
⅓ cup unsweetened applesauce

Preheat the oven to 350 degrees. Cut the ham into pieces and finely chop in a food processor. In a large skillet, heat the oil and cook the onion over medium heat until just softened, about 4 minutes. Add the apple and garlic and cook, stirring, for 2 minutes.

In a large mixing bowl, use your hands to gently but thoroughly combine the meat, bread crumbs, 2 tablespoons horseradish, mustard, thyme, caraway seeds, pepper, eggs, and ham. In a 13 by 9-inch baking pan, shape the meat into a 9 by 5-inch loaf or pat into a 9 by 5-inch loaf pan, smoothing the top. In a small bowl, stir together the applesauce and remaining 2 tablespoons horseradish. Spread over the top of the meatloaf.

Bake until the meatloaf is firm, rich golden brown, and a meat thermometer inserted into the center of the loaf registers 155 degrees, about 1 hour. Let the meatloaf stand in the pan for 10 minutes before slicing to serve.

Leftovers: Make cold sandwiches with sliced meatloaf, buttered rye bread, mustard, and lettuce.

Argentinian Steakloaf

6 servings

*A*rgentinian beef is excellent, and it is not uncommon in that country to find dishes that combine beef with hard-cooked eggs and other spicy ingredients. Here, the loaf slices prettily to show hard-cooked eggs that have been encased and insulated by the meat mixture during baking.

1 tablespoon olive oil
1 onion, chopped
½ red bell pepper, chopped
½ yellow bell pepper, chopped
2 cloves garlic, minced
½ teaspoon dried hot pepper flakes
1½ pounds ground sirloin or lean ground chuck
1 package (10 ounces) frozen chopped spinach, thawed and squeezed of all excess moisture

1 cup firm fresh white bread crumbs
¼ cup milk
1 egg
1 tablespoon grated orange zest
1 tablespoon chopped fresh oregano or 1 teaspoon dried
½ teaspoon hot pepper sauce
4 hard-cooked eggs, peeled

Preheat the oven to 350 degrees. In a large skillet, heat the oil and cook the onion and both bell peppers over medium-low heat, stirring occasionally, until the vegetables are just softened, about 4 minutes. Add the garlic and pepper flakes and cook 1 minute.

In a large mixing bowl, use your hands to gently but thoroughly combine the meat, spinach, bread crumbs, milk, egg, orange zest, oregano, pepper sauce, and cooked vegetables. Pat half of the meatloaf mixture into a 9 by 5-inch loaf pan. Arrange the eggs in a lengthwise row down the center, then pat the rest of the meatloaf mixture around and over the eggs.

Bake until the loaf is firm, the top is nicely browned, and a meat thermometer inserted into the center of the loaf registers 155 degrees, about 1 hour. Let the meatloaf stand for 10 minutes in the pan before slicing to serve hot.

Leftovers: Serve cold as part of a picnic platter that also includes potato salad and thickly sliced tomatoes.

Meatloaf Charmoula

6 servings

A spicy sauce from Morocco is the inspiration for the flavors in this meatloaf. I like it served with semolina bread and a big tossed salad.

Loaf
2 teaspoons olive oil
6 large cloves garlic, minced
¼ teaspoon dried hot pepper flakes
1½ pounds lean ground chuck
    or round
1 cup firm fresh sourdough or white
    bread crumbs
½ cup chopped cilantro
½ cup chopped flat-leaf parsley
2 tablespoons lemon juice
1 tablespoon grated lemon zest

1 tablespoon paprika
¾ teaspoon ground cumin
2 eggs
_____

Topping and Sauce
½ cup bottled chili sauce
½ cup regular or low-fat
    mayonnaise
2 tablespoons fresh lemon
    juice
1 teaspoon grated lemon zest
2 tablespoons chopped cilantro

Preheat the oven to 350 degrees.

For the meatloaf: In a small skillet over medium-low heat, warm the oil and cook the garlic and red pepper flakes for 1 minute, stirring constantly until just fragrant. In a large mixing bowl, use your hands to gently but thoroughly combine the meat, bread crumbs, cilantro, parsley, lemon juice and zest, paprika, cumin, eggs, and garlic mixture. In a 13 by 9-inch baking pan, shape the meat into a 9 by 5-inch loaf or pat it into a 9 by 5-inch loaf pan, smoothing the top.

For the topping and sauce: In a small bowl, stir together the chili sauce and mayonnaise. Spread about ⅓ cup of the mixture over the top of the meatloaf. Stir the lemon juice, zest, and cilantro into the remainder and reserve for the sauce.

Bake the meatloaf until it is firm, the top is richly browned, and a meat thermometer inserted into the center of the loaf registers 155 degrees, about 1 hour. Let stand 10 minutes in the pan before slicing to serve with the reserved sauce.

Leftovers: Serve cold slices on a bed of shredded romaine lettuce dolloped with additional sauce.

Beef and Gorgonzola Loaf

8 servings

*T*his is a richly flavored meatloaf that is wonderful served hot with Mushroom Marsala Sauce (page 150) or cold with just a dab of sour cream or mayonnaise.

1 tablespoon butter

1 small bunch arugula, coarsely chopped (about 1½ cups)

¼ cup finely chopped shallots

2 cloves garlic, minced

1½ pounds ground sirloin or lean ground chuck

1 cup firm fresh white bread crumbs

2 tablespoons cognac or brandy

2 tablespoons milk

1 tablespoon chopped fresh thyme or 1 teaspoon dried

1 egg

4 tablespoons bottled steak sauce

1 cup (4 ounces) crumbled Gorgonzola cheese

Preheat the oven to 350 degrees. In a large skillet, heat the butter and cook the arugula, shallots, and garlic over medium-low heat, stirring until the arugula is wilted, about 2 minutes.

In a large mixing bowl, use your hands to gently but thoroughly combine the meat, bread crumbs, cognac, milk, thyme, egg, 1 tablespoon of the steak sauce, and cooked vegetables. Mix in the cheese.

In a 13 by 9-inch baking pan, shape the meat into a 9 by 5-inch loaf, or pat it into a 9 by 5-inch loaf pan, smoothing the top. Spread the top with the remaining 3 tablespoons steak sauce. Bake about 1 hour until the loaf is firm, the top is richly browned, and a meat thermometer inserted into the center of the loaf registers 155 degrees. Let the meatloaf stand in the pan for 10 minutes before slicing to serve hot. If you want to serve this cold, let the meatloaf stand in the pan for 20 minutes, then invert onto a large piece of heavy-duty aluminum foil. Wrap well and refrigerate until cold, at least 2 hours or up to 36 hours, then slice and serve.

Leftovers: This makes an absolutely superb cold sandwich on thinly sliced brioche spread with grainy mustard and garnished with arugula leaves.

Osso Bucco Loaf with Gremolata Tomato Gravy

6 servings

*O*sso bucco is my favorite veal dish. The taste memory of fork-tender veal shanks braised with aromatic vegetables and the classic gremolata mix of lemon, garlic, and parsley are rekindled in this meatloaf.

1 tablespoon olive oil

2 carrots, coarsely chopped

1 medium onion, coarsely chopped

1 small fennel bulb, coarsely chopped

3 tablespoons minced garlic (about 6 cloves)

1 pound ground veal

½ pound ground beef chuck

1 cup day-old Italian bread crumbs

¾ cup chopped flat-leaf parsley

1 teaspoon salt

¾ teaspoon coarsely ground pepper

2 eggs

2 tablespoons grated lemon zest

1 can (14½ ounces) Italian-style stewed tomatoes

½ cup dry white wine

Preheat the oven to 350 degrees. In a large skillet, heat the oil and cook the carrots, onion, fennel, and 1 tablespoon of the minced garlic, partially covered, over medium-low heat until the vegetables are softened, about 5 minutes.

In a large mixing bowl, use your hands to gently but thoroughly mix together the veal, beef, bread crumbs, ½ cup of the parsley, salt, pepper, eggs, and about half of the cooked vegetables. (Reserve remaining vegetables in the skillet to use in the sauce.)

In a 13 by 9-inch baking pan, shape the meat into a 9 by 5-inch loaf or pat it into a 9 by 5-inch loaf pan, smoothing the top. Bake until the meatloaf is firm, the top is browned, and a meat thermometer inserted into the center of the loaf registers 155 degrees, about 1 hour.

While the meatloaf is baking, add the lemon zest, tomatoes with their juices, wine, remaining ¼ cup parsley, and remaining 2 tablespoons garlic to the vegetables in the skillet. Bring to a simmer and cook over medium-low heat, stirring occasionally, for 15 minutes until the sauce is slightly reduced.

Let the meatloaf stand in the pan for 10 minutes, then slice and serve with the sauce spooned over the top.

Sausage Ratatouille Loaf

6 servings

*E*ggplant, zucchini, onions, and bell peppers are available year round, as are canned tomatoes. So ratatouille, which is a classic summer dish, can be enjoyed even in the dead of winter. I often add spicy sausage to my ratatouille mixture, hence the idea for this meatloaf.

1 medium eggplant (about ¾ pound), peeled and sliced lengthwise slightly less than ¼ inch thick

2 tablespoons fruity olive oil

1 medium onion, chopped

1 small green bell pepper, diced

1 medium yellow summer squash or zucchini (about 6 ounces), diced

3 cloves garlic, minced

1 pound lean ground beef chuck

½ pound hot or sweet Italian sausage meat

1 cup firm fresh Italian bread crumbs

1 tablespoon chopped fresh oregano or 1 teaspoon dried

1 tablespoon chopped fresh thyme or 1 teaspoon dried

1 teaspoon salt

½ teaspoon freshly ground pepper

1 can (14 ounces) diced tomatoes and juice

¼ cup red wine

¼ cup chopped fresh basil

¼ teaspoon dried hot pepper flakes

Preheat the oven to 400 degrees. Arrange the eggplant slices in a single layer on a baking sheet. Brush with 1 tablespoon of the oil. Bake until the eggplant slices are tender, but not browned, about 10 minutes. Remove from the oven and reduce the heat to 350 degrees.

In a large skillet, heat the remaining 1 tablespoon oil and cook the onion, bell pepper, and squash over medium heat, stirring often, until the vegetables are just softened, about 4 minutes. Add the garlic and cook 1 minute.

In a large mixing bowl, use your hands to gently but thoroughly combine the beef, sausage, bread crumbs, oregano, thyme, salt, pepper, and cooked onion mixture. Place the meat in an elongated oval in a 13 by 9-inch baking dish. Form into an oval about 10 inches long and about 3 inches wide. Drape the eggplant slices crosswise over the meat.

In a small bowl, stir together the canned tomatoes with juice, wine, basil, and pepper flakes. Pour about half of the tomato mixture over the loaf.

Bake 30 minutes, then pour the remaining tomato mixture over the loaf. Bake an additional 20 minutes, then let stand for 10 minutes.

Serve the loaf in slices with the pan tomato sauce.

Leftovers: Serve cold slices on a bed of arugula topped with pesto thinned with enough mayonnaise for a thick, pourable sauce.

Sicilian Braciole Loaf

6 servings

*M*y aunt Margaret made the definitive braciole—at least as defined by our family. This meatloaf variation is a cousin to her recipe.

1 tablespoon olive oil
1 onion, chopped
1 large celery rib, chopped
1 carrot, chopped
2 cloves garlic, minced
1 pound lean ground chuck or
 ground round
½ pound ground veal
1 cup firm Italian bread crumbs,
 preferably from semolina bread
¼ cup grated Romano cheese
2 eggs

¾ teaspoon salt
½ teaspoon freshly ground pepper
¼ cup dried currants
¼ cup chopped flat-leaf parsley
1 tablespoon chopped fresh sage
 or 1 teaspoon dried
1 tablespoon chopped fresh
 marjoram or 1 teaspoon dried
1 teaspoon grated lemon peel
2 cups Mushroom Marsala Sauce
 (page 150) or bottled marinara
 sauce with mushrooms

Preheat the oven to 350 degrees. In a large skillet, heat the oil and cook the onion, celery, and carrot over medium-low heat, stirring often, until the vegetables are nearly softened, about 4 minutes. Add the garlic and cook, stirring, for 1 minute.

In a large mixing bowl, use your hands to gently but thoroughly mix together the ground meats, ¾ cup of the bread crumbs, cheese, eggs, salt, and pepper. On a large piece of waxed paper, pat the meat into a 9 by 12-inch rectangle. In a small mixing bowl, stir together the currants, parsley, sage, marjoram, lemon peel, and remaining ¼ cup bread crumbs. Sprinkle this filling over the meat, leaving a 1-inch border on all sides.

Use the waxed paper to help roll up the meat from the long side. Invert the roll into a 13 by 9-inch baking dish, discard the waxed paper, and smooth the edges of the meat to form a neat roll. Bake until the roll is firm and nicely browned, 45 to 50 minutes. While the loaf is baking heat the Mushroom Marsala Sauce or marinara sauce.

Let the meat roll stand for 10 minutes, then cut into 12 slices and serve with the sauce ladled over.

Pizza Rustica Loaf

6 servings

*W*ith cheese, sausage, pepperoni, and mushrooms, this is a pizza loaf with "the works." Serve it with crusty Italian bread.

1 pound lean ground beef chuck
½ pound hot or sweet Italian sausage meat
1 cup Italian bread crumbs
½ teaspoon salt
¼ teaspoon freshly ground pepper
1 egg

1 cup bottled marinara sauce with mushrooms
1 tablespoon olive oil
1 onion, thinly sliced
1 large clove garlic, minced
4 ounces thinly sliced mozzarella cheese
2 ounces very thinly sliced pepperoni

Preheat the oven to 375 degrees. In a large mixing bowl, use your hands to gently but thoroughly combine the beef, sausage, bread crumbs, salt, pepper, egg, and ¼ cup of the marinara sauce. Pat the mixture evenly to cover the bottom of a 13 by 9-inch baking dish. Bake 15 minutes.

Meanwhile, in a medium skillet, heat the oil and cook the onion and garlic over medium-low heat, stirring often, until the onion is very soft, about 10 minutes.

Spread the onion and the remaining ¾ cup marinara sauce over the partially cooked meat, then layer with the cheese and pepperoni.

Return to the oven and bake an additional 20 minutes until the cheese is melted and bubbly. Let the meatloaf stand for 5 to 10 minutes before cutting into squares to serve.

Leftovers: Reheat in the microwave oven and serve atop toasted Italian bread slices. Sprinkle with slivered basil and spoon additional heated marinara sauce over, if you wish.

Vitello Tonnato Loaf

8 servings

*T*hough this is just fine served hot from the oven, I really like it better cold, served in slices atop a bed of mixed summer lettuces garnished with tomato wedges and chilled, steamed green beans.

Tonnato Sauce
1 can (3½ ounces) tuna in olive oil, undrained
½ cup regular or low-fat mayonnaise
2 tablespoons fresh lemon juice
1 tablespoon small capers, drained
Loaf
1 tablespoon olive oil
2 carrots, chopped

1 onion, chopped
3 cloves garlic, minced
4 canned anchovies, drained
1 pound ground veal
½ pound lean ground chuck
1 cup fresh Italian bread crumbs
¼ cup chopped fresh basil
¼ cup chopped flat-leaf parsley
½ teaspoon dried hot pepper flakes
2 eggs

Make the tonnato sauce by draining the tuna and reserving 1 tablespoon of the oil. In a medium bowl, stir together the tuna, reserved oil, mayonnaise, lemon juice, and capers until blended and the tuna is crumbled but not mashed. Refrigerate at least 1 hour and up to 24 hours before using. Remove the sauce from the refrigerator and let stand at room temperature for 30 minutes before serving.

For the meatloaf: Preheat the oven to 350 degrees. In a large skillet, heat the oil and cook the carrots and onion over medium-low heat, stirring often, until the vegetables are just softened, about 4 minutes. Add the garlic and anchovies. Cook, stirring and mashing the anchovies with the back of a spoon, for 1 minute more.

In a large mixing bowl, use your hands to gently but thoroughly combine the veal, beef, bread crumbs, basil, parsley, pepper flakes, eggs, and cooked vegetables.

In a 13 by 9-inch baking pan, shape the meat into a 9 by 5-inch loaf, or pat it into a 9 by 5-inch loaf pan, smoothing the top. Bake until the loaf is firm, the top is richly browned, and a meat thermometer inserted into the center of the loaf registers 155 degrees, about 1 hour.

Let the meatloaf stand in the pan for 10 minutes before cutting to serve hot with tonnato sauce spooned over each slice.

Everybody Loves Meatloaf

Reuben Loaf

6 servings

*C*orned beef on rye with a little sauerkraut, Swiss cheese, and Thousand Island dressing, a classic Reuben, is my favorite sandwich. I like it as a meatloaf, too.

1 tablespoon vegetable oil
1 carrot, chopped
1 small onion, chopped
½ pound cooked corned beef
1 pound lean ground chuck
1 cup rye bread crumbs
½ cup well-drained sauerkraut

2 ounces Swiss cheese, cut into
  small cubes (about ½ cup)
½ cup prepared Thousand Island
  salad dressing
2 teaspoons dry mustard
½ teaspoon freshly ground pepper
1 egg

Preheat the oven to 350 degrees. In a medium skillet, heat the oil and cook the carrot and onion over medium-low heat until the vegetables are softened, about 5 minutes. Cut the corned beef into pieces and finely chop them in a food processor. In a large mixing bowl, use your hands to gently but thoroughly combine the ground chuck, bread crumbs, sauerkraut, cheese, ¼ cup of the Thousand Island dressing, mustard, pepper, egg, cooked vegetables, and corned beef.

Pat the mixture into a shallow 2-quart baking pan. Spread the top with the remaining ¼ cup Thousand Island dressing. Bake until the meatloaf is firm and the top is browned, 45 to 50 minutes. Let the meatloaf stand in the pan for 5 to 10 minutes before cutting into squares to serve.

Leftovers: Cut into slices and serve on toasted rye or pumpernickel bread with lettuce and more Swiss cheese and Thousand Island dressing.

Steak and Kidney Loaf

6 servings

A small amount of beef kidney lends richness and depth to meatloaf, almost turning it into pâté. A butcher will grind the kidneys for you, but if you truly loathe the idea of them you can simply use more ground chuck or try some ground venison. Frozen pearl onions are a great convenience and add real interest to this loaf.

1 tablespoon butter
½ pound (about 2 cups) frozen pearl onions
3 tablespoons cognac or brandy
2 tablespoons chopped fresh tarragon or 2 teaspoons dried
1¼ pounds lean ground chuck

¼ pound ground beef kidney
1 cup sourdough or French bread crumbs
1 tablespoon drained small capers
3 tablespoons Dijon mustard
1 teaspoon salt
1 teaspoon cracked black pepper

Preheat the oven to 350 degrees. In a large skillet, heat the butter over medium heat and cook the onions, stirring often, until they are golden brown and just tender, about 10 minutes. Add 2 tablespoons of the cognac and 1 tablespoon of the tarragon. Cook, stirring for 1 minute.

In a large mixing bowl, use your hands to gently but thoroughly combine the ground chuck, kidney, bread crumbs, remaining 1 tablespoon tarragon, capers, 1 tablespoon of the mustard, salt, pepper, and onions.

In a 13- by 9-inch baking pan, shape the meat into a 9 by 5-inch loaf, or pat it into a 9 by 5-inch loaf pan, smoothing the top. In a small bowl, stir together the remaining 1 tablespoon cognac and 2 tablespoons mustard. Brush the top of the loaf with the glaze.

Bake until the meatloaf is firm, richly browned, and a meat thermometer inserted into the center of the loaf registers 155 degrees, about 1 hour. Let the meatloaf stand in the pan for 10 minutes before slicing to serve.

Leftovers: Serve the cold meatloaf thinly sliced with plain wheat crackers or thin breads spread with mustard.

Everybody Loves Meatloaf

Thai Beef and Brown Rice Loaf

6 servings

*T*he lemongrass is optional, since it can be hard to find. Dried lemongrass is available, but grated lemon peel is an equally acceptable alternative. I like to serve these individual loaves hot over a bed of cold shredded lettuce that has been tossed with a sesame-soy vinaigrette.

⅓ cup uncooked brown rice (see Note)
1½ pounds lean ground chuck
1 cup thinly sliced scallions
¼ cup chopped fresh basil
2 tablespoons Thai fish sauce (nam pla)
2 tablespoons soy sauce

1 tablespoon chopped lemongrass or 1 teaspoon grated lemon peel
2 teaspoons sugar
2 cloves garlic, minced
1 teaspoon grated lime peel
1 teaspoon hot pepper sauce
¼ teaspoon dried hot pepper flakes
1 egg

In a small saucepan, bring 1 cup of lightly salted water to a boil. Add the rice, cover the pan, reduce the heat to low, and simmer until the rice is tender and the liquid is absorbed, about 35 minutes. (The rice can be cooked a day ahead and refrigerated.)

Preheat the oven to 350 degrees. In a large mixing bowl, use your hands to gently but thoroughly combine all of the ingredients, including the rice. Divide the mixture into 6 individual portions and place on a baking sheet. Form each portion into an oval about 4 inches long and 2½ inches high.

Bake until the loaves are firm and richly browned, 30 to 35 minutes.

Leftovers: Make sandwiches by cutting the meatloaf into chunks and rolling into flour tortillas spread with honey mustard and garnished with shredded lettuce.

Note: One cup cooked brown rice can be used here, and leftover white rice works fine, too.

Southwest Chorizo and Corn Bread Squares

6 servings

*Y*ou can use any corn bread or even nonsweet corn muffins for this loaf. If it is a very moist bread, crumble it onto a baking sheet and let it stand for several hours to dry out a bit.

1 pound "meatloaf mix" of ground chuck, pork, and veal

½ pound chorizo or spicy Italian sausage meat

1 cup firm fresh corn bread crumbs

1 cup fresh or thawed frozen or canned corn kernels, drained

1 cup thinly sliced scallions

⅓ cup chopped roasted red peppers, freshly roasted or from a jar

¼ cup chopped cilantro

2 teaspoons ground cumin

1 teaspoon salt

½ teaspoon freshly ground pepper

½ cup bottled salsa, plus additional for serving

Preheat the oven to 350 degrees. In a large mixing bowl, combine the meat, sausage, corn bread crumbs, corn, scallions, red pepper, cilantro, cumin, salt, and pepper. Pat the mixture into a shallow 2-quart baking pan. Spread the top with the ½ cup salsa.

Bake until the meatloaf is firm and the top is well browned, 45 to 50 minutes.

Let the meatloaf stand in the pan for 5 to 10 minutes before cutting into squares. While the meatloaf is standing, heat additional salsa in a small saucepan. Serve the meatloaf with the warm salsa.

Kids' Favorite Meatloaf

6 servings

*T*his is the easy way to get kids to eat their peas and carrots. A mildly flavored meatloaf with the slightly familiar cornflake taste topped with tomato ketchup is a guaranteed kid pleaser. (Adults will like it, too.)

1 tablespoon vegetable oil
1 onion, chopped
1 celery rib, chopped
1½ pounds "meatloaf mix" of
 ground chuck, pork, and veal
2 cups lightly crushed plain
 cornflakes cereal

1¾ cups (10-ounce package)
 thawed frozen peas and carrots
¼ cup chopped parsley
2 tablespoons Worcestershire sauce
1 tablespoon Dijon mustard
2 eggs
¼ cup ketchup

Preheat the oven to 350 degrees. In a large skillet, heat the oil and cook the onion and celery over medium-low heat, stirring often, until softened, about 5 minutes.

In a large mixing bowl, use your hands to gently but thoroughly combine the meat, cornflakes, peas and carrots, parsley, Worcestershire sauce, mustard, and eggs.

In a 13 by 9-inch baking pan, shape the meat into a 9 by 5-inch loaf, or pat it into a 9 by 5-inch loaf pan, smoothing the top. Spread the top with the ketchup. Bake until the meatloaf is firm with a richly browned top, and a meat thermometer inserted into the center of the loaf registers 155 degrees, about 1 hour.

Let the meatloaf stand in the pan for 10 minutes before slicing.

Leftovers: Make cold meatloaf sandwiches on good white bread with mustard or mayonnaise, lettuce, and sliced tomato. Serve with potato chips.

Grilled Meatloaves Provençal

6 servings

*T*f you don't have an extensive herb garden to flavor these
meatloaves, then substitute 1 tablespoon dried herbes de Provence, a
mixture that is readily available in the spice section of most grocery
stores. As with any dried herbs, store them in a cool, dark place and use
within a few months after opening the jar. The meatloaves can also be
baked in a traditional 9 by 5-inch loaf pan at 350 degrees for 1 hour.

2 teaspoons olive oil
1 cup thinly sliced leeks, white
*   part only*
¾ pound lean ground chuck
¾ pound ground veal
1 small bunch arugula, 6 leaves
*   reserved, the remainder chopped*
*   (about 1½ cups)*
1 cup French bread crumbs
¾ cup coarsely chopped roasted red
*   peppers, freshly roasted or from a*
*   jar*

¼ cup chopped fresh herbs (a
*   mixture of rosemary, marjoram,*
*   thyme, sage, savory, and anise or*
*   fennel fronds)*
1 teaspoon salt
¼ to ½ teaspoon dried hot pepper
*   flakes to taste*
1 egg
6 slices French bread
6 tomato slices
1 clove garlic, halved

Prepare a medium-hot barbecue fire or preheat a gas grill. On
the stove, in a medium skillet, heat the oil and cook the leeks over
medium heat until softened and pale golden, about 5 minutes. In a large
mixing bowl, use your hands to gently but thoroughly combine the
ground meats, chopped arugula, bread crumbs, roasted pepper, herbs,
salt, pepper flakes, egg, and leeks. Divide the mixture into 6 parts and
form into oval loaves, about 1 inch thick. Grill the meatloaves, turning
once or twice, until the exterior is well browned and the interior is no
longer pink, 14 to 18 minutes total.

While the meatloaves are grilling, set the bread slices and tomato
slices at the edge of the grill, and grill lightly on both sides, about
2 minutes. Rub one side of the toasts with the cut side of the garlic clove.
(Reserve remaining garlic for other uses.)

Serve the meatloaves on the toasts topped with the tomato and
reserved arugula leaves.

Barbecued Meatloaves

6 servings

*M*y mother invented barbecued meatloaves, or at least I hope that she did since I've been touting her recipe as the world's greatest with much success for many years now. Here is the latest version of her original.

1½ pounds "meatloaf mix" of ground chuck, pork, and veal
½ cup finely chopped sweet onion, such as Vidalia
½ cup firm fresh white bread crumbs
¼ cup chopped flat-leaf parsley
1 tablespoon Worcestershire sauce
1 tablespoon milk

1 teaspoon dry mustard
¾ teaspoon salt
½ teaspoon freshly ground pepper
¼ teaspoon freshly grated nutmeg
Pinch of ground cloves
1 egg
1 cup Barbecued Meatloaf Sauce (page 152) or bottled barbecue sauce

Prepare a medium-hot barbecue fire in a covered grill or preheat a gas grill.

In a large mixing bowl, use your hands to gently but thoroughly combine the meat, onion, bread crumbs, parsley, Worcestershire sauce, milk, mustard, salt, pepper, nutmeg, cloves, and egg. Form the mixture into 6 oval loaves, each about ¾ inch thick.

Grill the meatloaves, turning two or three times and brushing with the sauce halfway through the cooking, until the loaves are well browned and crisp on the outside and the meat is no longer pink in the center, about 15 minutes.

Leftovers: For barbecued meatloaf sandwiches, cut the loaves into chunks, then simmer for about 10 minutes in barbecue sauce thinned with a little beer or ginger ale. Serve on soft hamburger buns or white bread.

Meatloaf Pasties

6 servings

*T*he filling for pasties, traditional meat-filled pastry turnovers from Cornwall, England, is closely related to meatloaf.

1 cup plain low-fat yogurt
3 tablespoons grainy Dijon mustard
1 large waxy potato (about
* 6 ounces), peeled and diced*
3 small turnips (about 6 ounces),
* peeled and diced*
2 eggs
1½ pounds lean ground chuck
1 cup thawed frozen peas
* and carrots*

1 red onion, chopped
¼ cup chopped flat-leaf parsley
1 tablespoon chopped fresh savory
* or 1 teaspoon dried*
1 tablespoon chopped fresh thyme
* or 1 teaspoon dried*
1 teaspoon salt
½ teaspoon coarsely ground pepper
1 tube (10 ounces) refrigerated
* pizza dough*

In a small bowl, stir together the yogurt and mustard. Refrigerate at least 1 hour or overnight. (Return to room temperature to serve as a sauce for the pasties.)

Cook the potato and turnips in boiling salted water to cover until tender, about 8 minutes. Drain.

Preheat the oven to 350 degrees. In a large mixing bowl, whisk the eggs to blend. Pour about 1 tablespoon beaten egg into a small dish. Add 1 teaspoon water and whisk to blend. Reserve to use as glaze. To the egg in the large bowl, add the meat, peas and carrots, onion, parsley, savory, thyme, salt, pepper, and cooked vegetables. Use your hands to gently but thoroughly combine the ingredients. Divide into 6 portions.

Unwrap the pizza dough and use your hands to flatten it on a lightly floured surface to a rough 14-inch square. Cut into 6 equal pieces. Place 1 portion of the meat in the center of each dough piece. Fold the dough up and around the meat mixture to enclose it. Transfer the dough-wrapped meat to an ungreased baking sheet, smooth side up, leaving at least 2 inches in between each. Brush the tops of the pastries with the egg wash, then use a small knife to cut slits in each pastry portion.

Bake until the pastry is richly browned, about 40 minutes. Let stand 5 minutes before serving. Serve the hot pasties with the cool sauce.

Everybody Loves Meatloaf

Meatloaf en Croûte

6 servings

*R*emember beef Wellington? I liked it then, and I like it now (even though I've not seen it on a restaurant menu in fifteen years.) Maybe the meatloaf version will make it to a restaurant menu soon. If not, you can always order it at my house.

2 eggs
6 ounces mushrooms (a mix of wild and cultivated)
1 tablespoon butter
⅓ cup chopped shallots
1 tablespoon cognac or brandy
1½ pounds lean ground chuck

1 cup firm French bread crumbs
2 tablespoons chopped fresh tarragon or 1 teaspoon dried
1 teaspoon salt
½ teaspoon coarsely ground pepper
1 tube (10 ounces) refrigerated pizza dough

Preheat the oven to 350 degrees. In a large mixing bowl, whisk the eggs to blend. Pour about 1 tablespoon beaten egg into a small dish, add 1 teaspoon water, and whisk to blend. Reserve to use as glaze. Wipe the mushrooms clean with a damp paper towel, then trim and coarsely chop them. In a large skillet, heat the butter and cook the mushrooms over medium heat, stirring often, until softened, about 5 minutes. Add the shallots and cook, stirring often, until most of the mushroom liquid has evaporated, about 3 minutes more. Add the cognac and cook, stirring, for 1 minute.

In the bowl with the beaten eggs, add the meat, bread crumbs, tarragon, salt, pepper, and mushroom mixture. Use your hands to gently but thoroughly combine the ingredients. Divide into 6 portions.

Unwrap the pizza dough and use your hands to flatten it on a lightly floured surface to a rough 14-inch square. Cut into 6 equal pieces. Place 1 portion of the meat in the center of each dough piece. Fold the dough up and around the meat mixture to enclose it. Transfer the dough-wrapped meat to an ungreased baking sheet, smooth side up, leaving at least 2 inches in between each. Brush the tops of the pastries with the egg wash, then use a small knife to cut 2 slits in each.

Bake until the pastry is richly browned and the meat is no longer pink, about 40 minutes. Serve hot.

Venison and Wild Rice Loaf

6 servings

*V*enison is very lean, so if you want to substitute beef, be sure to get ground round or sirloin. This is a rather sophisticated loaf and I like it served with Cumberland Sauce (page 154) and some adult vegetables, such as buttered brussels sprouts and baked beets. If you have leftover cooked wild rice, use about 1 cup for this recipe.

⅓ cup uncooked wild rice
4 slices bacon
1 onion, finely chopped
1 carrot, finely chopped
3 cloves garlic, minced
2 tablespoons port wine
1 tablespoon crushed juniper
* berries or 2 tablespoons gin*

1 tablespoon chopped fresh
* rosemary or 1 teaspoon dried*
2 teaspoons dry mustard
1½ pounds ground venison
2 teaspoons grated fresh ginger
1 teaspoon salt
1 teaspoon cracked black pepper
2 eggs

In a small saucepan, bring 1 cup of lightly salted water to a boil. Add the rice, cover the pan, reduce the heat to low, and cook until the rice is tender and the liquid is absorbed, about 45 minutes. (The rice can be cooked a day ahead and refrigerated.)

Preheat the oven to 350 degrees. In a large skillet, partially cook the bacon until limp and some fat is rendered, 3 to 4 minutes. Remove the bacon from the skillet and add the onion and carrot. Cook over medium heat until the vegetables are just softened, about 4 minutes. Add the garlic and cook 1 minute. Remove from the heat and stir in the port wine, juniper berries or gin, rosemary, and mustard.

In a large mixing bowl, use your hands to gently but thoroughly combine the meat, ginger, salt, pepper, eggs, wild rice, and cooked vegetables.

In a 13 by 9-inch baking pan, shape the meat into a 9 by 5-inch loaf, or pat it into a 9 by 5-inch loaf pan, smoothing the top. Drape the bacon slices over the top. Bake until the meatloaf is firm, richly browned, and a meat thermometer inserted into the center of the loaf registers 155 degrees, about 1 hour.

Let the meatloaf stand in the pan for 10 minutes before slicing to serve.

Everybody Loves Meatloaf

Venison, Currant, and Wheat Bread Loaf

6 servings

*T*here are many good specialty wheat breads on grocery shelves these days. Cracked wheat is especially good in this loaf, but almost any multigrain loaf adds character to a meatloaf. If you can't get ground venison, use ground round or sirloin.

⅓ cup dried currants
2 tablespoons cognac or brandy
1 pound ground venison
½ pound ground pork
1 cup cracked wheat bread crumbs
1 celery rib, finely chopped
½ cup chopped shallots
½ cup chopped parsley
2 cloves garlic, minced

4 tablespoons tomato paste
4 teaspoons freshly grated or prepared horseradish
1 tablespoon chopped fresh thyme or 1 teaspoon dried
1 teaspoon salt
½ teaspoon coarsely ground black pepper
2 tablespoons currant jelly

Preheat the oven to 350 degrees. Soak the currants in the cognac for 15 minutes. In a large mixing bowl, use your hands to gently but thoroughly combine the venison, pork, bread crumbs, celery, shallots, parsley, garlic, 2 tablespoons of the tomato paste, 3 teaspoons of the horseradish, thyme, salt, pepper, and the soaked currants.

In a 13 by 9-inch baking pan, shape the meat into a 9 by 5-inch loaf, or pat it into a 9 by 5-inch loaf pan, smoothing the top. Bake for 30 minutes.

Meanwhile, in a small saucepan over low heat, melt the jelly with the remaining 2 tablespoons tomato paste and 1 teaspoon horseradish. After 30 minutes of baking, brush the top of the loaf with the glaze. Continue to bake another 30 minutes until the meatloaf is firm, the top is richly browned, and a meat thermometer inserted into the center of the loaf registers 155 degrees, about 1 hour.

Let the meatloaf stand in the pan for 10 minutes before slicing to serve.

Leftovers: Serve thinly sliced cold meatloaf with pickled beets, sliced hard-cooked eggs, and cornichons topped with a creamy mustard dressing.

Meat and Mustard Fruit Loaf

6 servings

*T*his is an exceptionally moist and rather sophisticated loaf. Serve it for an easy autumn Saturday night supper along with Slightly Lumpy Mashed Potatoes (page 158), steamed brussels sprouts tossed with a little browned butter, and an apple tart for dessert.

½ cup chopped packaged mixed dried fruit "bits"

¼ cup bourbon

1 pound lean ground pork

½ pound lean ground chuck

1 cup whole wheat bread crumbs

¼ cup minced shallots

3 tablespoons milk

2 eggs

1 tablespoon chopped fresh sage or 1 teaspoon dried

1 tablespoon chopped fresh thyme or 1 teaspoon dried

1 tablespoon dry mustard

1 teaspoon salt

½ teaspoon freshly ground pepper

¼ teaspoon ground mace

Preheat the oven to 350 degrees. Place the dried fruits and bourbon in a glass measuring cup or small dish. Cover and microwave just until very warm, about 1 minute. Let the fruits stand until the bourbon is absorbed, about 15 minutes.

In a large mixing bowl, use your hands to gently but thoroughly mix together the pork, beef, bread crumbs, shallots, milk, eggs, sage, thyme, mustard, salt, pepper, mace, and soaked fruits.

In a 13 by 9-inch baking pan, shape the meat into a 9 by 5-inch loaf, or pat it into a 9 by 5-inch loaf pan. Bake until the meatloaf is firm, the top is richly browned, and a meat thermometer inserted into the center of the loaf registers 155 degrees, about 1 hour.

Let the meatloaf stand 5 to 10 minutes in the pan, then slice to serve.

Leftovers: Reheat the slices in a microwave oven and serve topped with pan-fried sliced apples and onions.

Sage Sausage, Potato, and Apple Loaf

6 servings

*W*hen the weather turns cool, I like to serve this meatloaf with buttered cabbage and hunks of warm fresh bread or biscuits. If you have leftover baked potatoes or even sweet potatoes, you can use them in this recipe.

2 large waxy potatoes (about 12 ounces total), peeled and diced
1 pound lean ground pork
½ pound lean sage-seasoned pork sausage meat
¾ cup bran or whole wheat bread crumbs

⅔ cup unsweetened chunky applesauce
3 tablespoons Dijon mustard
1 red onion, chopped
1 tablespoon chopped fresh sage or 1 teaspoon dried

Cook the potatoes in boiling salted water to cover until they are tender, about 8 minutes. Drain well. (The potatoes can be cooked a day ahead and refrigerated.)

Preheat the oven to 350 degrees. In a large mixing bowl, use your hands to gently but thoroughly combine the pork, sausage meat, bran or bread crumbs, ⅓ cup of the applesauce, 1 tablespoon of the mustard, onion, sage, and potatoes.

In a 13 by 9-inch baking pan, shape the meat into a 9 by 5-inch loaf, or pat it into a 9 by 5-inch loaf pan. In a small bowl, stir together the remaining ⅓ cup applesauce and 2 tablespoons mustard. Brush over the top of the loaf.

Bake until the meatloaf is firm, the top is rich golden brown, and a meat thermometer inserted into the center of the loaf registers 155 degrees, about 1 hour.

Let the meatloaf stand 10 minutes in the pan before slicing to serve.

Leftovers: Heat slices in a microwave oven or in a skillet set over medium heat. Serve over a bed of wilted greens with a warm bacon dressing.

Basque-Style Meatloaf

6 servings

*O*ranges, olives, roasted peppers, and paprika are ingredients that immediately come to mind when I think of Spanish cooking. Combined with ground pork and ham, they make a great meatloaf.

½ pound smoked ham
1 pound lean ground pork
1 cup firm fresh sourdough or
*   crusty country bread crumbs*
½ cup green or black Spanish
*   olives, pitted and sliced*
1 small red onion, chopped
3 cloves garlic, minced
2 tablespoons tomato paste

1 tablespoon dry sherry
2 teaspoons paprika
1 teaspoon grated orange peel
2 eggs
1 cup sliced roasted red peppers,
*   freshly roasted or from a jar*
2 tablespoons orange marmalade
1 tablespoon red wine vinegar
*   or sherry*

Preheat the oven to 350 degrees. Cut the ham into chunks and finely chop in a food processor. In a large mixing bowl, use your hands to gently but thoroughly combine the pork, bread crumbs, olives, onion, garlic, tomato paste, sherry, paprika, orange peel, eggs, and ham. Pat half of the mixture into a 9 by 5-inch loaf pan. Make a layer of half of the roasted peppers, then pat the remaining meatloaf mixture over the peppers and top with the remaining peppers. In a small bowl, stir together the marmalade and vinegar. Brush over the top of the meatloaf and peppers.

Bake until the meatloaf is firm, the top is browned, and a meat thermometer inserted into the center of the loaf registers 155 degrees, about 1 hour.

Let the meatloaf stand for 10 minutes in the pan before slicing to serve.

Sweet and Sour Pork Loaf

6 servings

*F*resh ginger is one of my favorite seasonings. It has an affinity for everything from dim sum to desserts, so it shouldn't be a surprise that it does good things for meatloaf, especially this piquant pork and rice loaf.

1 tablespoon vegetable oil
1 large red bell pepper
1 cup thinly sliced scallions
3 cloves garlic, minced
2 tablespoons minced fresh ginger
2 tablespoons soy sauce
2 tablespoons prepared Chinese-
 style mustard

2 tablespoons rice wine vinegar
1½ pounds lean ground pork
¾ cup cooked white or brown rice
½ cup firm fresh white
 bread crumbs
2 eggs
½ cup crushed pineapple in juice
1 can (14½ ounces) diced tomatoes

Preheat the oven to 350 degrees. In a large skillet, heat the oil and cook the bell pepper over medium-low heat, stirring, until just softened, about 4 minutes. Stir in the scallions, garlic, and ginger and cook 1 minute more. Stir in the soy sauce, 1 tablespoon of the mustard, and 1 tablespoon of the vinegar. Transfer about three-quarters of the mixture to a large mixing bowl. Reserve remainder in skillet.

Add the pork, rice, bread crumbs, and eggs to the mixing bowl. Use your hands to gently but thoroughly mix the ingredients. In a 13 by 9-inch baking pan, shape the meat into a 9 by 5-inch loaf, or pat it into a 9 by 5-inch loaf pan, smoothing the top. Bake until the meatloaf is firm, the top is well browned, and a meat thermometer inserted into the center of the loaf registers 155 degrees, about 1 hour.

Meanwhile, reheat the mixture in the skillet. Stir in the pineapple and juice, tomatoes and juice, and the remaining 1 tablespoon mustard and 1 tablespoon vinegar. Simmer, stirring occasionally, for 10 minutes.

Let the meatloaf stand for 10 minutes before slicing and serving with the sauce.

Moo Shu Meatloaf

6 servings

*T*he original idea for this recipe came from Rick Rodgers's recipe in *365 Ways to Cook Hamburger and Other Ground Meats* (HarperCollins, 1992). Here is my expansion on this tasty theme.

6 ounces fresh shiitake mushrooms
1 tablespoon vegetable oil
2 cups thinly sliced napa
  cabbage
1 cup thinly sliced scallions
1 tablespoon finely chopped
  fresh ginger
2 cloves garlic, minced
1½ pounds lean ground pork

1 cup firm fresh white bread
  crumbs
1 tablespoon reduced-sodium
  soy sauce
2 tablespoons dry sherry
4 tablespoons hoisin sauce
1 teaspoon ground coriander
½ teaspoon crushed anise seeds
1 egg

Preheat the oven to 350 degrees. Wipe the mushrooms clean with damp paper towels, discard tough stems, and coarsely chop the mushrooms. In a large skillet, heat the oil and cook the mushrooms, stirring often over medium heat, until they are just softened, about 4 minutes. Add the cabbage and cook, stirring, until just wilted, about 2 minutes. Add the scallions, ginger, and garlic and cook 1 minute more.

In a large mixing bowl, use your hands to gently but thoroughly combine the meat, bread crumbs, soy sauce, 1 tablespoon of the sherry, 1 tablespoon of the hoisin sauce, coriander, anise seeds, egg, and cooked vegetables.

In a 13 by 9-inch baking pan, shape the meat into a 9 by 5-inch loaf, or pat it into a 9 by 5-inch loaf pan, smoothing the top. In a small dish, stir together the remaining 1 tablespoon sherry and 3 tablespoons hoisin sauce. Brush over the top of the meatloaf.

Bake until the meatloaf is firm, the top is well browned, and a meat thermometer inserted into the center of the loaf registers 155 degrees, about 1 hour.

Let the meatloaf stand in the pan for 10 minutes before slicing to serve.

Pork and Veal Rollatini

6 Servings

*T*his meatloaf is Italian comfort food. My aunt Margaret made it every time we came to visit. And we always felt comfortable at her table!

1 tablespoon olive oil
1 onion, chopped
1 large rib celery, chopped
3 cloves garlic, minced
¾ pound lean ground pork
¾ pound ground veal
1 cup firm Italian bread crumbs,
*   preferably semolina bread*
¼ cup slivered fresh basil leaves

1 tablespoon chopped fresh oregano
*   or 1 teaspoon dried*
2 eggs
4 ounces spinach leaves, lightly
*   steamed and well drained, or*
*   ½ cup thawed frozen leaf spinach,*
*   squeezed of excess moisture*
2 ounces very thinly sliced
*   prosciutto*

Preheat the oven to 350 degrees. In a large skillet, heat the oil and cook the onion and celery over medium heat, stirring often, until the vegetables are just softened, about 4 minutes. Add the garlic and cook 1 minute.

In a large mixing bowl, use your hands to gently but thoroughly combine the meats, bread crumbs, basil, oregano, eggs, and cooked vegetables. On a large piece of waxed paper, pat the meat mixture into a 9 by 12-inch rectangle. Make a layer of spinach, then a layer of prosciutto over the meat, leaving a 1-inch border all around. Use the waxed paper to help roll up the meat from the long side. Invert the roll into a 9 by 13-inch baking dish, discard the waxed paper, and smooth the meat to form a neat roll. Bake until the roll is firm and nicely browned, about 50 minutes.

Let stand about 10 minutes before cutting into slices.

Leftovers: Slice thinly and serve on crostini with a dab of pesto.

Ham and Pork Terrine
16 appetizer servings

*M*y culinary partner and friend, Brooke Dojny, considers this the "house pâté." She developed the amazingly easy recipe for our book *Parties!* and I credit her every time I serve my close adaptation as part of a party buffet. Garnish the platter with the classic cornichons, sliced radishes, and thin, crisp French bread toasts. The pâté is prettiest baked in a traditional mold, a long slim rectangular pan, but a loaf pan will work, too. If you are using a loaf pan, cut the slices in half to serve them.

4 ounces smoked ham, cut into
   ½-inch cubes
½ cup dried currants
1 cup port or Madeira wine
½ pound sliced bacon
2 eggs
½ cup light cream
2 tablespoons cognac or brandy
4 teaspoons chopped fresh thyme or
   1½ teaspoons dried

2 teaspoons salt
1 teaspoon freshly ground pepper
½ teaspoon ground allspice
¼ teaspoon freshly grated
   nutmeg
2 cloves garlic, minced
2 pounds lean ground pork
¼ pound chilled fresh pork fat,
   coarsely chopped
Coarsely ground black pepper

Combine the ham, currants, and port in a small bowl. Let stand 1 hour at room temperature.

Preheat the oven to 300 degrees. Completely line an 8-cup (9 by 5-inch) loaf pan or pâté mold with the bacon strips, reserving some strips for garnish.

In a small bowl, whisk the eggs with the cream and cognac. Add the thyme, salt, pepper, allspice, nutmeg, and garlic. Drain the ham and currants and add the soaking liquid to the egg mixture.

In a food processor, pulse to chop and combine the pork and pork fat. With the motor running, pour the egg mixture through the feed tube. Process to a smooth paste. Transfer the mixture to a bowl and stir in the reserved ham and currants.

Pat the mixture into the prepared pan. Lay reserved bacon strips over the top to enclose the meat. Cover the pan tightly with foil, place in a larger baking pan, and half fill the larger pan with hot water. Bake for

Everybody Loves Meatloaf

2 hours. Remove the foil and bake another 30 minutes, or until a meat thermometer inserted into the center of the loaf registers 155 degrees.

Remove the terrine from the water bath and cool for 30 minutes. Cover with foil. Place another slightly smaller pan on top of the foil and fill it with heavy cans to weight the terrine. Refrigerate overnight or up to 4 days.

To serve, scrape or peel off the bacon and discard. Invert the terrine on a platter. Peel off the bacon and sprinkle the top heavily with coarsely ground pepper. Cut into thin slices and arrange on a platter.

Meatloaf Tortière

6 servings

*T*n Quebec the meat pie called tortière is traditional holiday fare. This is an adaptation of the classic.

1 tablespoon vegetable oil
1 large onion, chopped
1 tart apple, peeled, cored, and chopped
1 tablespoon chopped fresh sage or 1 teaspoon dried
1 tablespoon chopped fresh thyme or 1 teaspoon dried
½ teaspoon ground cinnamon
¼ teaspoon ground cloves
2 eggs

1 pound lean ground pork
½ pound lean ground chuck
¾ cup cooked mashed potatoes
½ cup firm fresh white bread crumbs
¾ teaspoon salt
½ teaspoon freshly ground pepper
Pastry for a single-crust 10-inch pie or 1 disk from a 14-ounce package refrigerated piecrusts

Preheat the oven to 400 degrees. In a large skillet, heat the oil and cook the onion and apple over medium-low heat, stirring often, until the onion is almost softened, about 4 minutes. Stir in the sage, thyme, cinnamon, and cloves. Cook and stir for 1 minute. Remove the skillet from the heat and let the mixture cool.

In a large mixing bowl, beat the eggs, then remove 1 tablespoon of beaten eggs and reserve for an egg wash on the pastry. Add the pork, beef, mashed potatoes, bread crumbs, salt, pepper, and cooked onion-apple mixture to the remaining eggs in the mixing bowl. Use your hands to gently but thoroughly mix the meatloaf.

Pat the meatloaf into a 10-inch pie plate. If using homemade pie pastry, roll on a lightly floured surface to an 11-inch round. Place the homemade or purchased pastry disk on top of the meatloaf, crimping the edges against the rim of the dish. Use a small knife to make several slits in the pastry, then brush the pastry with the reserved beaten egg.

Bake the meatloaf for 30 minutes, then reduce the heat to 350 degrees and bake an additional 10 to 15 minutes until the pastry is rich golden. Let the meatloaf stand in the pan for 10 minutes, then cut into wedges to serve.

Pineapple Ginger Pork Squares

6 servings

*P*ineapple and ginger are pleasing partners with pork. Water chestnuts retain their crunch in the loaf, giving it an interesting texture. Reminiscent of traditional Chinese restaurant dishes, this is a meatloaf that the whole family will enjoy.

1 can (8 ounces) crushed pineapple in juice
1 tablespoon vegetable oil
1 green bell pepper, chopped
1 onion, chopped
1½ pounds lean ground pork
1 cup firm fresh white bread crumbs
¼ cup drained and coarsely chopped canned water chestnuts
2 tablespoons chopped cilantro
1½ tablespoons finely chopped fresh ginger
1 tablespoon reduced-sodium soy sauce
1½ teaspoons five-spice powder
1 egg
3 tablespoons prepared Chinese-style mustard

Preheat the oven to 350 degrees. Drain the pineapple, reserving the fruit and 2 tablespoons juice. In a large skillet, heat the oil and cook the pepper and onion over medium heat, stirring often, until the onion is golden, about 7 minutes.

In a large mixing bowl, use your hands to gently but thoroughly combine the meat, bread crumbs, water chestnuts, cilantro, ginger, soy sauce, five-spice powder, egg, pineapple, and cooked vegetables. Pat the mixture into a shallow 2-quart baking pan. In a small bowl, stir the mustard and reserved pineapple juice together. Brush over the top of the loaf.

Bake until the meatloaf is firm and the top is rich golden brown, 45 to 50 minutes.

Let the meatloaf stand in the dish for 5 to 10 minutes before cutting into squares to serve.

Leftovers: Cut the cold meatloaf into chunks and serve mixed into a rice salad dressed with a sesame-soy vinaigrette.

Ham and Spiced Sweet Potato Loaf

6 servings

*H*am is a wonderful ingredient in meatloaf, and the end result is directly related to the quality of ham that goes into the loaf. The sweet potato adds moisture, texture, and a touch of sweetness that nicely offsets the salty ham. Since this is a rather Southern meatloaf, serve it with boiled or sautéed greens and corn bread.

1 large sweet potato (about 8 ounces), peeled and diced (see Note)
½ pound smoked ham
1 pound lean ground pork
1 large sweet onion, such as Vidalia, chopped
1 cup whole wheat bread crumbs

¼ cup plain yogurt or sour cream
1 teaspoon grated orange peel
½ teaspoon ground allspice
¼ teaspoon freshly grated nutmeg
¼ teaspoon ground cloves
1 egg
2 tablespoons grainy Dijon mustard
2 tablespoons orange marmalade

Cook the sweet potato in lightly salted boiling water to cover until just tender, about 5 minutes. Drain well. Cut the ham into pieces and finely chop it in a food processor.

Preheat the oven to 350 degrees. In a large mixing bowl, use your hands to gently but thoroughly combine the pork, onion, bread crumbs, yogurt, orange peel, allspice, nutmeg, cloves, egg, sweet potatoes, and ham.

In a 13 by 9-inch baking pan, shape the meat into a 9 by 5-inch loaf, or pat it into a 9 by 5-inch loaf pan, smoothing the top. Bake for 20 minutes.

Meanwhile, in a small bowl, stir together the mustard and marmalade. After the meatloaf has baked for 20 minutes, spread or brush the glaze over the top. Continue to bake another 40 minutes until the loaf is firm, the top is rich golden brown, and a meat thermometer inserted into the center of the loaf registers 155 degrees.

Let the meatloaf stand in the pan for 10 minutes before slicing to serve.

Leftovers: Reheat slices and serve for breakfast with biscuits.

Ham, Hominy, and Bourbon Squares

6 servings

*D*on't be fooled by the down-home name of this meatloaf. It is very hot and spicy, so it is a perfect foil for soothing scalloped potatoes and a spinach salad. Canned hominy, which is corn treated with lime, makes a terrific meatloaf ingredient.

Loaf
½ pound smoked ham
1 pound lean ground pork
1 can (15 or 16 ounces) hominy,
  drained (about 1½ cups)
1 cup whole wheat bread crumbs
1 cup thinly sliced scallions
¼ cup bottled pickle relish
2 tablespoons maple syrup
2 tablespoons bourbon

1½ tablespoons hot pepper sauce
2 teaspoons dry mustard
2 eggs

_____

Maple Mustard Sauce
¼ cup Dijon mustard
3 tablespoons maple syrup
2 tablespoons white wine
  vinegar
1 tablespoon bourbon

Preheat the oven to 350 degrees.

For the meatloaf: Cut the ham into pieces and finely chop it in a food processor. In a large mixing bowl, use your hands to gently but thoroughly combine the pork, hominy, bread crumbs, scallions, relish, maple syrup, bourbon, pepper sauce, mustard, eggs, and ham. Pat the meatloaf into a shallow 2-quart baking dish. Bake until the meatloaf is firm, the top is rich golden brown, and a meat thermometer inserted into the center of the loaf registers 155 degrees, about 1 hour.

While the meatloaf is baking, make the sauce by combining all sauce ingredients in a small saucepan. Simmer, stirring often, until slightly reduced, about 3 minutes.

Let the meatloaf stand in the pan for 5 to 10 minutes before cutting into squares and serving with the sauce.

Leftovers: Serve cold squares on a bed of spinach and sliced red onion with a spoonful of room temperature maple mustard sauce.

Pork, Pear, and Smoked Gouda Loaves

6 servings

*A*lthough this loaf can be baked in a traditional loaf pan, I particularly like it as small individual loaves, where there is more of the fabulous glazed crust to encase the moist peppery meat mixture. The taste will vary according to the brand of sausage you use.

1 tablespoon vegetable oil
1 onion, chopped
1 ripe firm pear, peeled and diced
1 pound lean ground pork
½ pound lean breakfast
  sausage meat
1 cup firm white bread crumbs
1 tablespoon chopped fresh sage or
  1 teaspoon dried, crumbled

1½ teaspoons cracked black
  pepper
1 egg
3 ounces Gouda cheese, cut into
  ¼-inch cubes
3 tablespoons currant jelly
1 tablespoon prepared
  horseradish
2 teaspoons Dijon mustard

Preheat the oven to 400 degrees. In a large skillet, heat the oil and cook the onion over medium heat for 3 minutes, until just beginning to soften. Add the pear and cook 2 minutes, until the pear is softened.

In a large mixing bowl, use your hands to gently but thoroughly combine the pork, sausage meat, bread crumbs, sage, pepper, egg, and cooked onion and pear. Add the cheese and mix to combine. Divide the mixture into 6 portions and place on a large baking sheet. Form each portion into an oval about 4 inches long and 2½ inches high.

In a small saucepan over medium-low heat, melt the jelly with the horseradish and mustard. Brush the meatloaves with the glaze. Bake until the loaves are firm and richly browned, 30 to 35 minutes.

Leftovers: Slice the cold meatloaf and serve on a bed of mixed greens accompanied by sliced pears and small wedges of smoked Gouda cheese.

Ham, Lima Bean, and Corn Bread Loaf

6 servings

*A*ll the ingredients of a good Southern Sunday supper combine in this meatloaf—in fact the recipe comes from an old Carolina friend who makes it on Mondays from the Sunday leftovers. Her whole family comes back for supper on Monday. She says they like the "leftover loaf" better than the original supper.

1/2 pound smoked ham
1 pound lean ground pork
1 cup cooked baby lima beans
1 cup corn bread crumbs
1 cup cooked corn kernels
1 cup thinly sliced scallions
1/2 cup chopped celery
2 tablespoons chopped fresh thyme
*   or 2 teaspoons dried*

1 tablespoon chopped fresh savory
*   or 1 teaspoon dried*
1 tablespoon hot pepper sauce
1 teaspoon ground celery seed
1/2 teaspoon salt
1/2 teaspoon freshly ground
*   pepper*
2 eggs
1/4 cup ketchup

Preheat the oven to 350 degrees. Cut the ham into pieces and finely chop in a food processor. In a large mixing bowl, use your hands to gently but thoroughly combine the pork, lima beans, corn bread crumbs, corn, scallions, celery, thyme, savory, pepper sauce, celery seed, salt, pepper, eggs, and ham.

In a 13 by 9-inch baking pan, shape the meat into a 9 by 5-inch loaf, or pat it into a 9 by 5-inch loaf pan, smoothing the top. Spread the top with the ketchup. Bake until the meatloaf is firm, the top is richly browned, and a meat thermometer inserted into the center of the loaf registers 155 degrees, about 1 hour. Let the meatloaf stand in the pan for 10 minutes before slicing to serve.

Leftovers: Make sandwiches on white bread with mustard and shredded lettuce.

Barbecued Porkloaves on Buns

6 servings

*C*arolina pork barbecue is made from fork-tender shreds of highly seasoned pork shoulder sloshed with a peppery vinegar sauce and served heaped onto a soft bun along with a spoonful of coleslaw. This meatloaf recalls those same flavors, with some of the coleslaw in the meatloaf mixture to add texture and moistness.

1½ pounds lean ground pork
1 cup firm fresh white bread crumbs
1⅔ cups creamy coleslaw
1 onion, chopped
1 tablespoon chopped fresh thyme or 1 teaspoon dried
1 tablespoon hot pepper sauce

¾ teaspoon salt
½ teaspoon coarsely ground pepper
½ teaspoon ground celery seed
1 egg
2 tablespoons Worcestershire sauce
6 soft hamburger buns or 12 slices white bread

Prepare a medium-hot barbecue fire or preheat a gas grill. In a large mixing bowl, use your hands to gently but thoroughly combine the pork, bread crumbs, ⅓ cup of the coleslaw, onion, thyme, pepper sauce, salt, pepper, celery seed, and egg. Divide the mixture into 6 portions and form each into an oval loaf about ¾ inch thick. Brush the loaves with the Worcestershire sauce.

Grill the loaves, turning once or twice, until they're well browned on the outside and the meat is no longer pink, about 15 minutes.

Serve the meatloaves and remaining coleslaw on the buns.

Italian Easter Loaf

6 servings

*M*eat pies are a part of the Italian Easter feast, especially as cold fare on the picnics that are traditional on Easter Monday, which is a holiday throughout Italy. This is definitely not a traditional version, but it is wonderful on Easter Monday or any Monday, hot or cold. Spring onions look like fat scallions, but taste more like leeks, so they are the best substitute.

2 teaspoons olive oil
1 cup thinly sliced spring onions or slender leeks, white part only
2 cloves garlic, minced
1 pound lean ground lamb
½ pound hot or sweet Italian sausage meat
1 cup Italian bread crumbs
½ cup low-fat ricotta cheese
¼ cup chopped flat-leaf parsley
3 tablespoons chopped fresh basil or 2 teaspoons dried

2 tablespoons chopped fresh oregano or 1½ teaspoons dried
1 teaspoon salt
½ teaspoon freshly ground pepper
1 egg
1 can (1 pound) artichoke hearts, drained and quartered, or 1 package (9 ounces) frozen artichoke hearts, cooked and quartered

Preheat the oven to 350 degrees. In a medium skillet, heat the oil and cook the spring onions over medium-low heat until softened, about 5 minutes. Add the garlic and cook 1 minute. In a large mixing bowl, use your hands to gently but thoroughly combine the lamb, sausage, bread crumbs, ricotta, parsley, basil, oregano, salt, pepper, egg, and leeks. Add the artichokes and mix in gently so that they do not break apart.

Pat the mixture into a 9-inch round cake pan that is at least 2 inches deep or a 2-quart shallow baking pan. Bake until the meatloaf is firm and the top is richly browned, 45 to 50 minutes. Let the meatloaf stand in the pan for at least 5 to 10 minutes before cutting into wedges or squares to serve.

Leftovers: This is often served cold, in wedges or squares set on a bed of arugula along with roasted pepper strips and sweet onion slices, and a dab of aioli or garlicky mayonnaise.

Mediterranean Lamb, Goat Cheese, and Sun-Dried Tomato Loaf

6 servings

*G*round lamb is common in many Mediterranean cuisines. It is flavorful enough to stand up to assertive goat cheese and sun-dried tomatoes, and is also a wonderful foil for the sweet pungency of roasted garlic and onions. Pita bread, with its firm texture, makes excellent bread crumbs.

1 medium onion, cut into 8 wedges
4 large cloves garlic, peeled
1 tablespoon extra-virgin olive oil
1 ounce packaged sun-dried tomatoes (about ¼ cup)
1½ pounds lean ground lamb
1 cup whole wheat or white pita bread crumbs

¼ cup chopped flat-leaf parsley
½ teaspoon ground coriander
½ teaspoon salt
½ teaspoon freshly ground pepper
2 eggs
¾ cup (3 ounces) crumbled goat cheese

Preheat the oven to 350 degrees. Place the onion wedges and garlic cloves on a double thickness of aluminum foil. Drizzle with the oil, then wrap the onion and garlic in the foil to seal well. Roast the vegetables for 25 to 30 minutes until very tender. Remove from the oven and as soon as they are cool enough to handle, coarsely chop the onion and garlic. Do not turn off the oven.

While the vegetables are roasting, reconstitute the tomatoes by placing them in a small bowl, then pouring boiling water to cover over them. Let stand until softened, about 20 minutes. Drain the tomatoes, then chop them.

In a large mixing bowl, use your hands to gently but thoroughly mix together the lamb, pita bread crumbs, parsley, coriander, salt, pepper, eggs, chopped sun-dried tomatoes, and roasted vegetables. Add the goat cheese and mix again just until the cheese is incorporated but retains its crumbly texture.

In a 13 by 9-inch baking pan, shape the meat into a 9 by 5-inch loaf, or pat it into a 9 by 5-inch loaf pan, smoothing the top. Bake until the meatloaf is firm, the top is richly browned, and a meat thermometer inserted into the center of the loaf registers 155 degrees, about 1 hour. Let the meatloaf stand 10 minutes in the pan, then slice to serve.

Leftovers: Serve cold chunks stuffed into pita pockets dolloped with plain yogurt. Garnish with chopped tomato and cilantro.

Shepherd's Pie Loaf
with Port Gravy

*T*he classic English shepherd's pie is made from leftover cooked lamb or beef, gravy, vegetables, and topped with mashed potatoes. The concept is just as delicious as a meatloaf, baked in a dish so that it can be cut into attractive squares and served with the rich port wine gravy. Steamed sugar snap peas and sautéed cherry tomatoes tossed with herbs are colorful accompaniments.

2 tablespoons butter

3 carrots, coarsely chopped

2 celery ribs, coarsely chopped

2 cups thinly sliced leeks, white and pale green parts only

2 tablespoons chopped fresh savory or 2 teaspoons dried

6 tablespoons port wine

¾ pound extra-lean ground chuck

¾ pound lean ground lamb

1 cup firm fresh white bread crumbs

6 tablespoons chopped flat-leaf parsley

¾ teaspoon salt, plus additional to taste

½ teaspoon freshly ground black pepper, plus additional to taste

½ teaspoon ground allspice

2 eggs

3 cups cooked mashed potatoes

1 tablespoon all-purpose flour

1¼ cups reduced-sodium canned beef broth

Preheat the oven to 375 degrees. In a large skillet, heat the butter and cook the carrots, celery, and leeks over medium-low heat, stirring often until vegetables are softened, about 5 minutes. Stir in the savory and 2 tablespoons of the port.

In a large mixing bowl, use your hands to gently but thoroughly mix together the beef, lamb, bread crumbs, 4 tablespoons of the parsley, ¾ teaspoon salt, ½ teaspoon pepper, allspice, and eggs. Add about two-thirds of the sautéed vegetable mixture, leaving the remainder in the skillet to use for the gravy. Use your hands to gently but thoroughly mix the meatloaf.

Pat the meatloaf into a shallow 2-quart baking pan. Gently spread the mashed potatoes over the meatloaf. (If the potatoes are cold, they may be too stiff to spread. Reheat gently in a microwave oven or stir a little warm milk into the potatoes until they are thick, but spreadable.)

Bake the meatloaf until it is firm and the potatoes are pale golden, about 50 minutes.

While the meatloaf is baking, reheat the vegetables in the skillet. Stir in the flour and cook over medium heat, stirring, for 2 minutes. Whisk or gradually stir in the broth and remaining 4 tablespoons port. Cook, stirring, until the gravy is thickened and comes to a boil. Stir in the remaining 2 tablespoons parsley and simmer 2 minutes, stirring. Season to taste with salt and pepper.

Serve the meatloaf cut into squares with the gravy spooned over the top.

Lamb and Lentil Loaf

6 servings

*L*entils are a wonderful "filler" for meatloaves, providing both flavor and texture. This rather exotic and spicy loaf makes a fine informal supper, accompanied by a tomato and cucumber salad, Indian flat breads, and perhaps a little rosewater-scented custard for dessert.

1 cup dried brown or green lentils
2 cups canned vegetable broth
  or water
2 teaspoons olive oil
1 onion, chopped
1 pound lean ground lamb
1 package (9 ounces) frozen
  chopped spinach, thawed and
  squeezed of all excess water

1 cup firm white bread crumbs
2 teaspoons grated lemon peel
2 teaspoons grated orange
  peel
1 teaspoon salt
1 teaspoon ground cinnamon
½ teaspoon ground cloves
½ teaspoon cayenne
2 eggs

Place the lentils and broth in a medium saucepan. Cover the pan, bring to a boil, reduce the heat to low, and cook, covered, until the lentils are tender, about 30 minutes. Drain off any excess liquid.

Preheat the oven to 350 degrees. In a medium skillet, heat the oil and cook the onion over medium heat, stirring often, until the onion is golden, about 7 minutes. In a large mixing bowl, use your hands to gently but thoroughly combine the lamb, spinach, bread crumbs, lemon and orange peels, salt, cinnamon, cloves, cayenne, eggs, lentils, and onion.

In a 13 by 9-inch baking pan, shape the meat into a 9 by 5-inch loaf, or pat it into a 9 by 5-inch loaf pan, smoothing the top. Bake until the meatloaf is firm, the top is richly browned, and a meat thermometer inserted into the center of the loaf registers 155 degrees, about 1 hour. Let the meatloaf stand for 10 minutes before slicing to serve.

Leftovers: Serve at room temperature on a bed of spinach leaves dolloped with yogurt mixed with a little chopped cilantro.

Kibbeh Loaf

6 servings

*K*ibbeh, a classic Middle Eastern dish, can be prepared in many ways, but traditional preparations almost always include bulgur and lamb in a crust or coating that encloses a spiced lamb and nut filling. This is a very simplified meatloaf-style version.

Bulgur Layer
1¼ cups bulgur
¾ pound lean ground lamb
½ cup minced onion
½ teaspoon salt
¼ teaspoon cayenne
Filling
½ pound lean ground lamb
1 onion, chopped

2 cloves garlic, minced
½ teaspoon salt
½ teaspoon ground cinnamon
½ teaspoon ground coriander
¼ teaspoon ground allspice
¼ teaspoon freshly ground pepper
⅓ cup chopped cilantro
¼ cup coarsely chopped
    pistachio nuts

For the bulgur layer: In a medium pan, bring 2 cups of lightly salted water and the bulgur to a boil over medium-high heat. Reduce the heat to low, cover the pot, and simmer until the liquid is absorbed by the bulgur, 15 to 20 minutes. Spoon the bulgur into a mixing bowl and let it cool. (The bulgur can be cooked a day ahead and refrigerated or you can use 2 cups of leftover cooked bulgur.) Add the lamb, onion, salt, and cayenne and mix well to thoroughly combine. Reserve while making the filling.

For the filling: In a large skillet, cook the lamb, onion, garlic, salt, cinnamon, coriander, allspice, and pepper over medium heat, stirring occasionally, until the lamb loses its pink color and the onion is softened, 6 to 8 minutes. Drain off excess fat. Stir in the cilantro.

Preheat the oven to 350 degrees. Pat about half of the bulgur-lamb mixture into the bottom of a 2-quart baking dish. Spread all of the cooked lamb filling over the shell, then make a top layer by patting the remaining bulgur-lamb mixture over the cooked lamb. Sprinkle with the pistachios.

Bake until the top of the kibbeh is richly browned and crisp, 40 to 50 minutes. Let the kibbeh stand for 10 minutes, then cut into squares.

Barbecued Lamb Koftas

6 servings

*T*hese spicy individual loaves have a wonderfully crunchy crust and a moist, flavorful interior. The minted yogurt garnish provides a cooling counterpoint.

1½ cups plain low-fat yogurt
3 tablespoons chopped fresh mint
1½ pounds lean ground lamb
1 cup fresh firm white bread
   crumbs
1 cup thinly sliced scallions
3 cloves garlic, minced
2 tablespoons curry powder

1 tablespoon ground cumin
1 tablespoon ground coriander
1 teaspoon salt
½ teaspoon cayenne
¼ cup golden raisins
1 tablespoon chopped fresh
   ginger
1 cup alfalfa sprouts

In a small bowl, stir 1 cup of the yogurt and the mint together. Let stand 30 minutes at room temperature, or refrigerate up to 4 hours before using.

Prepare a medium-hot barbecue fire or preheat a gas grill. In a large mixing bowl, use your hands to combine the meat, bread crumbs, scallions, garlic, curry powder, cumin, coriander, salt, cayenne, raisins, ginger, and remaining ½ cup yogurt. Divide the mixture into 6 portions and form into oval loaves, each about 1 inch thick.

Grill the meatloaves, turning once or twice, until the exterior is well browned and crisp and the interior is no longer pink, 15 to 18 minutes.

Serve the meatloaves dolloped with the minted yogurt and sprinkled with sprouts.

Poultry Loaves

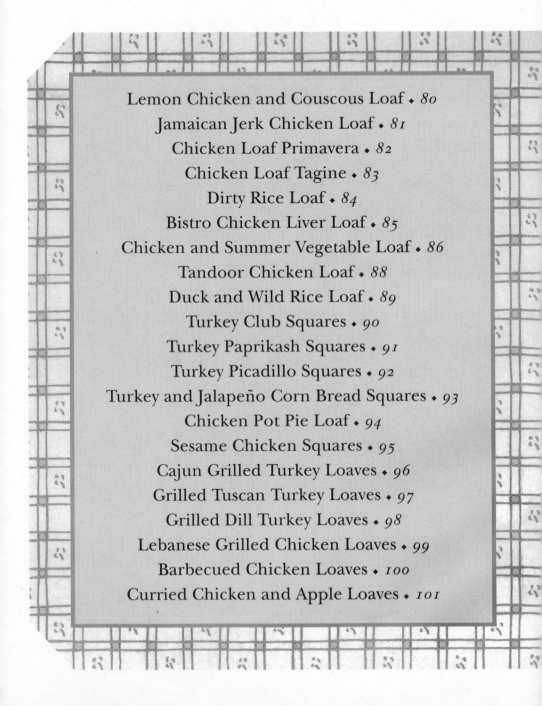

Poultry Loaves

Chicken may be America's favorite food. Judging by the size of the chicken department in any market, it's clear that we are buying birds as fast as they fly into the store. But, in recent years, chicken has had to move over to make way for its bigger cousin, turkey. This bird, which used to enjoy our attention only on Thanksgiving and as the day-after sandwich, has, through good breeding and promotion, become a year-round favorite. Like the chicken, turkey is available whole or in parts. But turkey's best contribution to everyday dining may be in ground form. (In this area, chicken has had to play catch-up, but it is increasingly available.)

Lower in fat than ground meat, home cooks and recipe writers alike use ground turkey as a meatloaf alternative, sometimes with real success but other times with dismally dry results. As I tinker with turkey, I find that the basic taste is fine but the texture is enhanced by a bit more filler and a lot of herbs or spices. Ground chicken is even more tender than turkey, but this quality makes a spectacular, delicate mousselike loaf. In most recipes, turkey and chicken are interchangeable, but note that the chicken will usually produce a moister, softer loaf.

Ground turkey and chicken are good red meat alternatives, but they are also eminently worthy to stand on their own merits.

Truck-Stop Turkey Loaf

6 servings

T've eaten meatloaf in more truck stops than I can remember. And the first turkey loaf that I ever ate was in a truck stop in Indiana. This was a cutting-edge truck stop with a computerized sign, but we stopped there anyway since it passed my grandma's ten-trucks-in-the-parking-lot rating test. The turkey loaf was excellent and it opened a whole new world of meatloaf variations for me. Like this loaf, the truck stop was simple and old-fashioned but with a few modern ideas.

1½ pounds ground turkey
1 onion, finely chopped
1 cup uncooked quick oats
½ cup chopped flat-leaf
  parsley
⅓ cup milk
½ cup bottled chili sauce

2 tablespoons chopped fresh thyme
  or 2 teaspoons dried
1 teaspoon salt
½ teaspoon freshly ground pepper
1 egg
Herbed Chicken Gravy (page 149),
  optional

Preheat the oven to 350 degrees. In a large mixing bowl, use your hands to gently but thoroughly combine the turkey, onion, oats, parsley, milk, ¼ cup of the chili sauce, thyme, salt, pepper, and egg.

In a 13 by 9-inch baking pan, shape the mixture into a 9 by 5-inch loaf or pat it into a 9 by 5-inch loaf pan, smoothing the top. Spread the remaining ¼ cup chili sauce over the top.

Bake until the loaf is firm, the top is browned, and a meat thermometer inserted into the center of the loaf registers 160 degrees, about 1 hour. Let the meatloaf stand in the pan for 10 minutes before slicing to serve with Herbed Chicken Gravy, if desired.

Leftovers: Make classic meatloaf sandwiches on white bread with mayonnaise, lettuce, and tomato.

Turkey and Sage Stuffing Loaf

6 servings

*T*his is unbelievably easy and good, offering all the tastes of Thanksgiving for only a few minutes' work.

1 tablespoon vegetable oil
1 onion, chopped
1 celery rib, chopped
1½ pounds ground turkey
1 cup crushed dry herb-seasoned
*   stuffing mix*

½ teaspoon salt
½ teaspoon freshly ground pepper
2 eggs
1 cup canned whole berry
*   cranberry sauce*
2 tablespoons prepared horseradish

Preheat the oven to 350 degrees. In a medium skillet, heat the oil and cook the onion and celery over medium heat, stirring often, until the vegetables are softened, about 5 minutes.

In a large mixing bowl, use your hands to gently but thoroughly combine the turkey, stuffing mix, salt, pepper, eggs, and cooked vegetables.

In a 13 by 9-inch baking pan, shape the mixture into a 9 by 5-inch loaf, or pat it into a 9 by 5-inch loaf pan, smoothing the top. In a small bowl, stir together the cranberry sauce and horseradish. Spread about one-third of the mixture over the meatloaf.

Bake until the loaf is firm, the top is richly browned, and a meat thermometer inserted into the center of the loaf registers 160 degrees, about 1 hour. Let the loaf stand in the pan for 10 minutes before slicing to serve with the remaining cranberry-horseradish sauce.

Leftovers: Make cold meatloaf sandwiches on white bread with more cranberry-horseradish sauce and lettuce.

Turkey and Sun-Dried Tomato Pesto Loaf

6 servings

*T*f you love pesto, then this is your loaf. I like slices served on a bed of vermicelli with Meatloaf Marinara Sauce (page 153) or a good-quality bottled marinara sauce. If you want a really peppery meatloaf, use the greater amount of hot pepper flakes.

¼ cup pine nuts

*⅔ cup drained and chopped
oil-packed sun-dried tomatoes
(reserve 1 tablespoon of oil)*

4 cloves garlic, minced

1½ pounds ground turkey

*2 cups chopped fresh arugula leaves
(about 1 large bunch)*

1 cup Italian bread crumbs

½ cup chopped fresh basil

*¼ cup grated Parmesan
cheese*

½ teaspoon salt

*¼ to ½ teaspoon dried hot
pepper flakes*

1 egg

Preheat the oven to 350 degrees. In a small dry skillet, toss the pine nuts over medium heat until they are golden and fragrant, 3 to 4 minutes. Add the reserved sun-dried tomato oil and garlic and cook, stirring, for 1 minute. Remove the pan from the heat.

In a large mixing bowl, use your hands to gently but thoroughly combine the turkey, arugula, bread crumbs, basil, cheese, salt, pepper flakes, egg, pine nut mixture, and sun-dried tomatoes.

In a 13 by 9-inch baking pan, shape the mixture into a 9 by 5-inch loaf, or pat it into a 9 by 5-inch loaf pan, smoothing the top.

Bake until the loaf is firm, the top is richly browned, and a meat thermometer inserted into the center of the loaf registers 160 degrees, about 1 hour. Let the loaf stand in the pan for 5 to 10 minutes before cutting into slices to serve.

Leftovers: Make hot meatloaf hero sandwiches by reheating chunks of meatloaf in marinara sauce, then ladling onto split hero or submarine rolls. Add shredded lettuce, if desired.

Sauerkraut and Turkey Kielbasa Loaf

6 servings

*K*ielbasa, or Polish-style smoked sausage, has long been available made from pork or beef, but turkey kielbasa is a relative newcomer to the market. It is lower in fat than traditional kielbasa but has all of the flavor. Along with sauerkraut and ground turkey, kielbasa makes an unusual but most delicious meatloaf.

½ pound turkey kielbasa or smoked sausage
1 tablespoon vegetable oil
1 onion, chopped
1 pound ground turkey
1½ cups well-drained sauerkraut
1 cup rye bread crumbs

½ cup chopped flat-leaf parsley
1½ tablespoons paprika
1 teaspoon caraway seeds
½ teaspoon salt
½ teaspoon freshly ground pepper
1 egg
¼ cup unsweetened applesauce

Preheat the oven to 350 degrees. Cut the kielbasa into chunks, then finely chop it in a food processor. In a medium skillet, heat the oil and cook the onion over medium heat until softened, about 5 minutes. In a large mixing bowl, use your hands to gently but thoroughly combine the ground turkey, sauerkraut, bread crumbs, parsley, paprika, caraway seeds, salt, pepper, egg, chopped kielbasa, and cooked onion.

In a 13 by 9-inch baking pan, shape the mixture into a 9 by 5-inch loaf, or pat it into a 9 by 5-inch loaf pan, smoothing the top. Spread the applesauce over the top.

Bake until the loaf is firm, the top is richly browned, and a meat thermometer inserted into the center of the loaf registers 160 degrees, about 1 hour. Let the meatloaf stand in the pan for 10 minutes before slicing to serve.

Leftovers: Serve slices or chunks cold on a bed of bitter greens with a creamy horseradish dressing or a Thousand Island dressing.

Turkey and Shiitake Loaf
with Sherry Gravy

6 servings

*T*he mushrooms are in both the meatloaf and the gravy, which once again proves that you can't get too much of a good thing. Curry paste is available at Asian or Indian markets and at many grocery stores.

3 tablespoons vegetable oil
1 pound fresh or 3 ounces dried and reconstituted shiitake mushrooms, trimmed and coarsely chopped
2 carrots, diced
1 cup chopped scallions
2 tablespoons chopped fresh ginger
3 tablespoons nam pla (Thai fish sauce)
2 tablespoons soy sauce

1½ pounds ground turkey
1 cup firm fresh whole wheat bread crumbs
1 cup cooked brown or white rice
2 tablespoons prepared green curry paste
2 eggs
1 tablespoon sesame seeds
1 cup reduced-sodium chicken broth
1 tablespoon cornstarch
3 tablespoons dry sherry

In a large skillet, heat the oil and cook the mushrooms and carrots over medium heat, stirring often, until the mushrooms and carrots are soft, about 8 minutes. Add the scallions, ginger, nam pla, and soy sauce. Cook 2 minutes. Spoon about half of the mushroom mixture into a large mixing bowl and leave the remainder in the skillet.

To the mushrooms in the mixing bowl, add the turkey, bread crumbs, rice, curry paste, and eggs. Use your hands to gently but firmly combine the ingredients.

In a 13 by 9-inch baking pan, shape the mixture into a 9 by 5-inch loaf, or pat it into a 9 by 5-inch loaf pan, smoothing the top. Sprinkle with the sesame seeds.

Bake the loaf until it is firm, the top is richly browned, and a meat thermometer inserted into the center of the loaf registers 160 degrees, about 1 hour. Let the meatloaf stand in the pan for 10 minutes before slicing to serve.

While the meatloaf is baking, make the gravy. Add the chicken broth to the mushroom mixture reserved in the skillet. Bring to a boil.

Everybody Loves Meatloaf

In a small bowl, dissolve the cornstarch in the sherry and whisk into the mushroom mixture. Bring to a boil, stirring constantly. Cook until the mushroom gravy is slightly thickened, about 1 minute.

Serve the meatloaf slices covered with the gravy.

Leftovers: Reheat meatloaf chunks and any leftover gravy and toss into cooked rice along with chopped scallions and a tablespoon of soy sauce.

Heritage Turkey and Chestnut Loaf

6 servings

*M*y family heritage encompasses both Italian and Pennsylvania Dutch, a combination that leads to some really eclectic holiday meals. Christmas could be turkey with both chestnut stuffing and an herbed bread (both sides of the family like chestnuts). Here is an amalgam of these flavors in a really good meatloaf.

1 tablespoon olive oil
1 onion, chopped
1 carrot, chopped
2 cloves garlic, minced
¼ cup dry white wine
1½ pounds ground turkey
1 cup diced cooked chestnuts
  (see Note)
1 cup Italian bread crumbs
⅓ cup chopped flat-leaf parsley

1 tablespoon chopped fresh
  marjoram or 1 teaspoon dried
1 tablespoon chopped fresh thyme
  or 1 teaspoon dried
¾ teaspoon salt
½ teaspoon grated nutmeg
¼ teaspoon dried hot pepper flakes
¼ teaspoon freshly ground
  black pepper
2 eggs

Preheat the oven to 350 degrees. In a medium skillet, heat the oil and cook the onion and carrot over medium heat, stirring, until the onion is just softened, about 4 minutes. Add the garlic and cook 1 minute. Add the wine and boil, stirring often, until most of the liquid has evaporated, about 3 minutes.

In a large mixing bowl, use your hands to gently but thoroughly combine the turkey, chestnuts, bread crumbs, parsley, marjoram, thyme, salt, nutmeg, pepper flakes, black pepper, eggs, and cooked vegetables.

In a 13 by 9-inch baking pan, shape the mixture into a 9 by 5-inch loaf, or pat it into a 9 by 5-inch loaf pan. Bake the loaf until it is firm, the top is richly browned, and a meat thermometer inserted into the center of the loaf registers 160 degrees, about 1 hour. Let the meatloaf stand in the pan for 10 minutes before slicing to serve.

Note: You can cook fresh chestnuts, use canned chestnuts, or reconstitute dried chestnuts for this recipe. Do not use sweetened chestnuts in syrup, however.

Tarragon Turkey Hash Loaf

6 servings

*I*f we still have leftover Thanksgiving turkey in the refrigerator on Saturday morning, we usually make hash for breakfast. Actually, we like hash so much that we buy a turkey big enough to ensure adequate "leftovers." The transition from Saturday-morning hash to Saturday-night meatloaf was an easy one, indeed.

4 slices bacon, cut in half
1 onion, chopped
1 small red bell pepper, chopped
2 cups diced cooked waxy potatoes
*   (about 2 potatoes)*
1½ pounds ground turkey
1 cup firm white bread crumbs or
*   herb-seasoned stuffing mix*

1 cup cooked green peas
⅓ cup chopped flat-leaf parsley
2 tablespoons chopped fresh
*   tarragon or 1½ teaspoons dried*
1 teaspoon paprika
1 teaspoon salt
½ teaspoon freshly ground pepper
2 eggs

Preheat the oven to 350 degrees. In a large skillet, cook the bacon until limp and some of the fat is rendered. Remove the bacon from the skillet, leaving about 2 tablespoons drippings in the skillet. Add the onion and bell pepper to the drippings and cook over medium heat until just softened, about 3 minutes. Raise the heat to medium-high, add the potato, and cook, stirring often, until the vegetables are just golden, about 5 minutes.

In a large mixing bowl, use your hands to gently but thoroughly combine the turkey, bread crumbs, peas, parsley, tarragon, paprika, salt, pepper, eggs, and cooked vegetables.

Pat the mixture into a shallow 2-quart baking pan. Lay the partially cooked bacon slices over the top. Bake the loaf until it is firm, the top is richly browned, and a meat thermometer inserted into the center of the loaf registers 160 degrees, 45 to 50 minutes.

Let the meatloaf stand in the baking dish for 5 to 10 minutes before cutting into squares to serve.

Leftovers: Reheat in a microwave and serve on a bed of steamed greens topped with a spoonful of stewed tomatoes.

Turkey Loaf Lindstrom

6 servings

*T*his combination of vegetables and herbs appears in several variations in many of my Scandinavian cookbooks, and they always seem to be called "Lindstrom." Unable to obtain an accurate assessment of its origins, I simply adapted Lindstrom to a meatloaf and it has become a family favorite at my house.

1 tablespoon vegetable oil
1 onion, chopped
1 cup diced cooked waxy potato (about 1 large potato)
1¼ pounds ground turkey
¼ pound chicken livers, finely chopped by hand or in a food processor
1 cup rye bread crumbs

6 tablespoons sour cream, regular or reduced-fat
3 tablespoons chopped fresh dill
1 teaspoon salt
½ teaspoon freshly ground pepper
1 egg
1 cup diced cooked beets (about 3 small beets)
3 tablespoons grainy Dijon mustard

Preheat the oven to 350 degrees. In a medium skillet, heat the oil and cook the onion over medium heat, stirring often, until the onion is just softened, about 3 minutes. Raise the heat to medium-high, add the potatoes, and cook, stirring often, until the potatoes and onions are just golden, about 4 minutes.

In a large mixing bowl, use your hands to gently but thoroughly combine the ground turkey, livers, bread crumbs, 4 tablespoons of the sour cream, dill, salt, pepper, egg, and the cooked onions and potatoes. Gently mix in the beets.

Pat the mixture into a shallow 2-quart baking pan. In a small bowl, stir together the mustard and remaining 2 tablespoons sour cream. Spread over the top of the loaf. Bake until the loaf is firm, the top is browned, and a meat thermometer inserted into the center of the loaf registers 160 degrees, 45 to 50 minutes.

Let the meatloaf stand in the baking dish for 5 to 10 minutes before cutting into squares to serve.

Leftovers: Reheat and serve over wide egg noodles tossed with butter and parsley.

Turkey Scrapple Loaf

6 servings

*S*crapple is a Philadelphia staple, and is one of those dishes that tastes far better than it sounds. This meatloaf is proud of its Pennsylvania scrapple heritage of cornmeal, livers, and herbs.

2 teaspoons vegetable oil
1 onion, chopped
½ pound ground turkey
½ pound turkey breakfast sausage meat
¼ pound chicken livers, finely chopped by hand or in a food processor
2 cups finely crumbled day-old corn bread

¼ cup prepared mincemeat
2 tablespoons chopped fresh sage or 2 teaspoons dried
2 tablespoons chopped fresh thyme or 2 teaspoons dried
2 teaspoons cracked black pepper
¾ teaspoon salt
2 eggs

Preheat the oven to 350 degrees. In a medium skillet, heat the oil and cook the onion over medium heat, stirring often, until softened, about 5 minutes. In a large mixing bowl, use your hands to gently but thoroughly combine the ground turkey, sausage, livers, corn bread, mincemeat, sage, thyme, pepper, salt, eggs, and onion.

In a 13 by 9-inch pan, shape the mixture into a 9 by 5-inch loaf, or pat it into a 9 by 5-loaf pan, smoothing the top.

Bake until the loaf is firm, the top is richly browned, and a meat thermometer inserted into the center of the loaf registers 160 degrees, about 1 hour. Let the meatloaf stand in the pan for 10 minutes before cutting into slices to serve.

Leftovers: Broil thin slices until a bit crusty, then serve for breakfast with pancakes and maple syrup.

Turkey Mole Loaf

6 servings

*L*ittle did the nuns in Mexico realize that they were inventing a national classic when they scrambled to pull together a celebratory meal from herbs, spices, and pantry staples for an unexpected visit from the bishop. And they surely could not have envisioned that their wonderful mole sauce would inspire a meatloaf. Thanks, sisters.

1 tablespoon vegetable oil
1 onion, chopped
3 tablespoons sesame seeds
3 cloves garlic, minced
2 tablespoons chili powder
1 teaspoon ground cumin
1½ pounds ground turkey
1 cup coarsely crushed baked tortilla chips

½ cup tomato sauce
½ teaspoon ground cinnamon
½ teaspoon ground coriander
½ ounce unsweetened chocolate, grated
1 jalapeño pepper, seeded and chopped
1 egg

Preheat the oven to 350 degrees. In a medium skillet, heat the oil and cook the onion, stirring often over medium heat, until just softened, about 4 minutes. Add the sesame seeds, garlic, chili powder, and cumin. Cook, stirring, for 2 minutes, until seeds and garlic are lightly toasted.

In a large mixing bowl, use your hands to gently but thoroughly combine the turkey, tortilla chips, tomato sauce, cinnamon, coriander, chocolate, jalapeño, egg, and onion mixture.

In a 13 by 9-inch baking pan, shape the mixture into a 9 by 5-inch loaf, or pat it into a 9 by 5-inch loaf pan, smoothing the top.

Bake until the loaf is firm, the top is richly browned, and a meat thermometer inserted into the center of the loaf registers 160 degrees, about 1 hour. Let the meatloaf stand in the pan for 10 minutes before slicing to serve.

Leftovers: Serve cold on a bed of greens topped with corn relish and/or tomato salsa.

Basque Chicken and Olive Loaf

6 servings

*S*ince they are the predominant flavor, use good-quality black or green olives, preferably those from the Mediterranean, for this recipe. Roasted peppers from a jar are a fine convenience product, especially when they are chopped to be incorporated into the loaf anyway.

1¼ pounds ground chicken
1 cup peasant or other coarse bread crumbs
1 cup diced cooked waxy potato (1 large potato)
1 cup diced smoked ham (about 4 ounces)
¾ cup chopped roasted red peppers, freshly roasted or from a jar
¾ cup chopped red onion

¾ cup chopped pitted black or green olives, or a combination
½ cup chopped flat-leaf parsley
½ cup toasted chopped almonds
1 tablespoon red wine vinegar
½ teaspoon cayenne
1 egg
Lemon-Caper Sour Cream (page 156)

Preheat the oven to 350 degrees. In a large mixing bowl, use your hands to gently but thoroughly combine the chicken, bread crumbs, potato, ham, roasted pepper, onion, olives, parsley, ¼ cup of the almonds, vinegar, cayenne, and egg.

In a 13 by 9-inch baking pan, shape the mixture into a 9 by 5-inch loaf, or pat it into a 9 by 5-inch loaf pan, smoothing the top. Sprinkle with the remaining ¼ cup almonds.

Bake until the loaf is firm, the top is richly browned, and a meat thermometer inserted into the center registers 160 degrees, about 1 hour. Let the meatloaf stand in the pan for 10 minutes before cutting into slices to serve with Lemon-Caper Sour Cream.

Leftovers: Serve cold with more Lemon-Caper Sour Cream.

Lemon Chicken and Couscous Loaf

6 servings

*T*he lemon and mint make a sprightly, summery meatloaf that is good hot or cold. The traditional Moroccan seasonings give it just a bit of an exotic twist, but it has a wide appeal that makes it a favorite among children, too.

1½ pounds ground chicken
1 cup cooked couscous, cooked according to package directions
1 cup firm fresh white bread crumbs
1 cup chopped scallions
1 package (9 ounces) frozen chopped spinach, thawed and squeezed of excess water

1 tablespoon grated lemon peel
⅓ cup chopped fresh mint
1 teaspoon ground coriander
1 teaspoon salt
½ teaspoon freshly ground black pepper
¼ teaspoon cayenne
1 egg

Preheat the oven to 350 degrees. In a large mixing bowl, use your hands to gently but thoroughly combine all of the ingredients.

In a 13 by 9-inch baking pan, shape the mixture into a 9 by 5-inch loaf, or pat it into a 9 by 5-inch loaf pan, smoothing the top.

Bake until the loaf is firm, the top is browned, and a meat thermometer inserted into the center of the loaf registers 160 degrees, about 1 hour.

Let the meatloaf stand in the pan for 10 minutes before slicing to serve.

Leftovers: Serve cold stuffed into pita breads garnished with plain yogurt, alfalfa sprouts, and diced tomato.

Jamaican Jerk Chicken Loaf

6 servings

*T*he hot and spicy mix of seasonings that comprises a traditional jerk marinade or rub enhance meatloaf, too. The starchy rice and beans temper the peppery heat, but you can also vary the amount of jalapeños and cayenne according to your taste, then team the meatloaf with a cooling salad that highlights tropical fruits.

1½ pounds ground chicken
1 cup cooked white rice
1 cup rinsed and drained canned
   black beans
1 cup thinly sliced scallions
½ cup firm white bread crumbs
2 tablespoons lime juice
1 to 2 tablespoons seeded and
   minced fresh or pickled jalapeño
   peppers
3 cloves garlic, minced

2 teaspoons grated lime peel
2 tablespoons chopped fresh thyme
   or 2 teaspoons dried
2 tablespoons chopped fresh sage or
   1½ teaspoons dried
1 teaspoon salt
¾ teaspoon ground allspice
½ teaspoon cayenne
½ teaspoon ground cinnamon
1 egg
3 tablespoons jalapeño jelly

Preheat the oven to 350 degrees. In a large mixing bowl, use your hands to gently but thoroughly combine the ground chicken, rice, beans, scallions, bread crumbs, lime juice, jalapeños, garlic, lime peel, thyme, sage, salt, allspice, cayenne, cinnamon, and egg.

In a 13 by 9-inch baking pan, shape the mixture into a 9 by 5-inch loaf, or pat it into a 9 by 5-inch loaf pan, smoothing the top. In a small saucepan or in a microwave oven, heat the jelly until melted, then spread it over the top of the loaf.

Bake until the loaf is firm, the top is richly browned, and a meat thermometer inserted into the center of the loaf registers 160 degrees, about 1 hour. Let the meatloaf stand in the pan for 10 minutes before slicing to serve.

Leftovers: Make sandwiches on Italian bread spread with mayonnaise mixed with a little jalapeño jelly. Add shredded lettuce or sprouts.

Chicken Loaf Primavera

6 servings

*A*lmost any cooked vegetables from sliced asparagus to diced zucchini will work in this meatloaf. Tarragon is an herb that fairly sings springtime, while I think basil says summer and dill reminds me of cool weather. So if you make this when it isn't "primavera," change the herbs according to the season.

1½ pounds ground chicken
1 cup firm white bread crumbs
1 cup cooked baby peas
1 cup diced cooked carrots
1 cup chopped watercress
½ cup chopped red onion
½ cup light cream or milk
2 tablespoons Dijon mustard

2 tablespoons chopped fresh
tarragon or 1 teaspoon dried
2 tablespoons snipped fresh chives
plus 8 whole chives for garnish
¾ teaspoon salt
½ teaspoon freshly ground pepper
½ teaspoon grated nutmeg
1 egg

Preheat the oven to 350 degrees. In a large mixing bowl, use your hands to gently but thoroughly combine the ground chicken, bread crumbs, peas, carrots, watercress, onion, cream, mustard, tarragon, snipped chives, salt, pepper, nutmeg, and egg.

In a 13 by 9-inch baking pan, shape the mixture into a 9 by 5-inch loaf, or pat it into a 9 by 5-inch loaf pan, smoothing the top. Crisscross the whole chives over the loaf.

Bake until the loaf is firm, the top is browned, and a meat thermometer inserted into the center of the loaf registers 160 degrees, about 1 hour. Let the meatloaf stand in the pan for 10 minutes before slicing to serve.

Leftovers: Make sandwiches on white toast with herbed mayonnaise and watercress sprigs.

Chicken Loaf Tagine

6 servings

*T*he spiced vegetable-accented tagines of Morocco are the inspiration for this meatloaf. In fact, it makes good use of leftover cooked vegetables and couscous. If you don't have eggplant and zucchini, substitute other summer squashes and cooked bell peppers.

2 tablespoons olive oil

1 small eggplant (about ½ pound), peeled and cut into ½-inch dice

1 medium zucchini (about 6 ounces), cut into ½-inch dice

1 onion, chopped

3 cloves garlic, minced

1½ pounds ground chicken

1 cup cooked couscous

1 cup firm white bread crumbs

½ cup chopped flat-leaf parsley

⅓ cup chopped cilantro

1 tablespoon grated fresh ginger

2 teaspoons grated lemon peel

2 teaspoons grated orange peel

1 teaspoon ground cumin

1 teaspoon salt

½ teaspoon freshly ground pepper

¼ teaspoon cayenne

¼ teaspoon ground cinnamon

1 egg

Preheat the oven to 350 degrees. In a large skillet, heat the oil and cook the eggplant, zucchini, onion, and garlic over medium-low heat, covered, stirring occasionally, until the vegetables are very soft, 12 to 15 minutes. In a large mixing bowl, use your hands to gently but thoroughly combine the chicken, couscous, bread crumbs, parsley, cilantro, ginger, lemon and orange peels, cumin, salt, pepper, cayenne, cinnamon, egg, and cooked vegetables.

In a 13 by 9-inch baking pan, shape the mixture into a 9 by 5-inch loaf, or pat it into a 9 by 5-inch loaf pan, smoothing the top.

Bake until the loaf is firm, the top is richly browned, and a meat thermometer inserted into the center of the loaf registers 160 degrees, about 1 hour. Let the meatloaf stand in the pan for 10 minutes before slicing to serve.

Leftovers: Stuff cold slices or chunks into pita breads. Garnish with plain yogurt and radish sprouts.

Dirty Rice Loaf

6 servings

*N*o, dirty rice is not like dirty laundry. It's a classic Louisiana dish of rice and chicken livers along with lots of herbs and spices. The chicken livers may muddy up the color of the rice, but they do great things for the flavor! Chicken livers are a fine ingredient to enrich poultry loaves, too.

1 tablespoon vegetable oil
1 onion, chopped
1 celery rib, chopped
½ green bell pepper, chopped
2 cloves garlic, minced
1 tablespoon chili powder
1 teaspoon ground cumin
¾ pound ground turkey
½ pound turkey or beef chorizo sausage meat

¼ pound chicken livers, finely chopped by hand or in a food processor
1 cup cooked white rice
1 cup firm white bread crumbs
2 teaspoons hot pepper sauce
½ teaspoon salt
2 eggs
⅓ cup ketchup

Preheat the oven to 350 degrees. In a large skillet, heat the oil and cook the onion, celery, and green pepper, stirring often over medium heat, until the vegetables are softened, about 5 minutes. Stir in the garlic, chili powder, and cumin, and cook for 1 minute.

In a large mixing bowl, use your hands to gently but thoroughly combine the ground turkey, chorizo, livers, rice, bread crumbs, pepper sauce, salt, eggs, and cooked vegetables.

In a 13 by 9-inch baking pan, shape the mixture into a 9 by 5-inch loaf, or pat it into a 9 by 5-inch loaf pan, smoothing the top. Spread the ketchup over the loaf.

Bake until the loaf is firm, the top is richly browned, and a meat thermometer inserted into the center of the loaf registers 160 degrees, about 1 hour. Let the meatloaf stand in the pan for 10 minutes before slicing to serve.

Leftovers: Reheat and serve over rice with Cajun-style stewed tomatoes.

Bistro Chicken Liver Loaf

6 servings

*T*his rich loaf is more like a country pâté and is good in thin slices atop a bed of leafy greens or lightly buttered fettuccine. Serve it cold with traditional pâté accoutrements, such as plain toasts, cornichons, capers, chopped red onion, and a dab of sour cream or yogurt. The loaf can be baked in small pans, chilled, then wrapped in plastic, and given as gifts.

1 tablespoon butter

1 onion, chopped

½ pound smoked ham, cut into ¼-inch dice

1 pound ground chicken or turkey

½ pound chicken livers, finely chopped by hand or in a food processor

1 cup firm French bread crumbs

¼ cup heavy cream

3 tablespoons scotch whiskey

3 tablespoons rinsed and drained green peppercorns, packed in brine

2 tablespoons chopped fresh thyme or 2 teaspoons dried

½ teaspoon ground allspice

½ teaspoon freshly ground pepper

¼ teaspoon salt

1 egg

Preheat the oven to 350 degrees. In a medium skillet, heat the butter over medium heat and cook the onion and ham, stirring often, until the onion is softened and the ham is browned, about 5 minutes.

In a large mixing bowl, use your hands to gently but thoroughly combine the ground chicken, livers, bread crumbs, cream, whiskey, peppercorns, thyme, allspice, pepper, salt, egg, and cooked onion and ham.

In a 13 by 9-inch baking pan, shape the mixture into a 9 by 5-inch loaf, or pat it into a 9 by 5-inch loaf pan, smoothing the top.

Bake until the loaf is firm, the top is richly browned, and a meat thermometer inserted into the center of the loaf registers 160 degrees, about 1 hour. Let the meatloaf stand in the pan for 10 minutes before slicing to serve.

Chicken and Summer Vegetable Loaf

6 servings

*A*dmittedly rich, this "mosaic" of vegetables and diced ham in a smooth chicken loaf is a close adaptation of a chilled terrine recipe in Brooke Dojny's and my book *Parties!* With a few small proportion changes, the loaf can be served hot from the oven as a chicken loaf or cold as a terrine. Both options are given. Tomato-Citrus Chutney (page 156) or pesto sauce are good accompaniments, whether the loaf is hot or cold.

¾ cup diced carrots
1 cup green peas, freshly shelled or frozen
¾ cup diced red bell pepper
1½ pounds ground chicken
1 egg

1½ cups chilled heavy cream
⅓ cup thinly sliced scallions
1 teaspoon salt
½ teaspoon grated nutmeg
½ teaspoon ground white pepper
1 cup diced smoked ham

Preheat the oven to 350 degrees. Butter a 9 by 5-inch loaf pan. In a medium saucepan, cook the carrots and peas in boiling salted water to cover for 30 seconds. Add the bell pepper and cook for 2 minutes. Drain the vegetables in a colander, then rinse under cold water to set the color. Drain well on a paper towel.

Place the ground chicken and egg in a food processor. With the motor running pour the cream through the feed tube to make a smooth thick puree. Transfer the mixture to a bowl and stir in the scallions, salt, nutmeg, pepper, ham, and cooked vegetables.

Spoon the mixture into the prepared pan, smoothing the top. Lay a sheet of buttered parchment or waxed paper over the chicken mixture and cover tightly with foil. Place the loaf pan in a larger baking pan. Add hot water to the baking pan to come halfway up the sides of the loaf pan. Bake until the loaf is firm and an instant read thermometer inserted into the center of the loaf registers 160 degrees, about 1½ hours. Let the meatloaf stand in the pan for at least 20 minutes, then drain off any excess liquid. Cut into slices to serve warm. If you want to serve this cold, cover the top of the loaf in the pan with plastic wrap. Place another loaf pan directly on top of the loaf and weight the top pan with heavy cans. (This will compact the loaf and make it easy to slice thinly to serve cold.) Refrigerate for at least 4 hours or up to 48 hours before slicing to serve.

Leftovers: Serve the cold loaf in thin, overlapping slices on a bed of tender summer greens.

Tandoor Chicken Loaf

6 servings

*A*tandoor is an Indian clay oven, and not a specific dish. Though I have never seen meatloaf on an Indian menu, the fabulous flavors that comprise many tandoori marinades work wonders in regular ovens and with meatloaves, too. Serve it with Cucumber-Yogurt Sauce (page 155), sliced tomatoes, Indian flat breads, and a rosewater-scented custard for a very sophisticated yet simple meal.

2 tablespoons vegetable oil
2 carrots, chopped
1 onion, chopped
1 large celery rib, chopped
1 tablespoon curry powder
1 teaspoon salt
1 teaspoon ground coriander
1 teaspoon ground cumin
½ teaspoon ground allspice
½ teaspoon turmeric

½ teaspoon ground mace
½ teaspoon ground cardamom
1½ pounds ground chicken
1 cup cooked white rice
1 cup firm fresh white bread crumbs
¼ cup chopped dried bananas
   (see Note)
¼ cup chopped cilantro
¼ cup plain yogurt
2 eggs

Preheat the oven to 350 degrees. In a large skillet, heat the oil and cook the carrots, onion, and celery over medium heat, stirring often, until the vegetables are softened, about 5 minutes. Stir in the curry powder, salt, coriander, cumin, allspice, turmeric, mace, and cardamom.

In a large mixing bowl, use your hands to gently but thoroughly combine the chicken, rice, bread crumbs, bananas, cilantro, yogurt, eggs, and cooked vegetables.

In a 13 by 9-inch baking pan, shape the mixture into a 9 by 5-inch loaf, or pat it into a 9 by 5-inch loaf pan, smoothing the top.

Bake until the loaf is firm, the top is richly browned, and a meat thermometer inserted into the center of the loaf registers 160 degrees, about 1 hour. Let the meatloaf stand in the pan for 10 minutes before cutting into slices to serve.

Note: Dried bananas are available in packages in the dried fruit section of many supermarkets or in health food stores.

Duck and Wild Rice Loaf
6 servings

*T*f you don't want to use duck in this recipe, substitute ground turkey for the duck and chicken livers for the duck liver. If you can get the butcher to grind turkey thigh meat for you, all the better since it has a richer, more gamelike flavor. Cooked brown rice can replace wild rice, if necessary.

¼ cup dried cherries

¼ cup diced dried apricots

¼ cup Madeira wine or dry sherry

2 tablespoons red wine vinegar

2 teaspoons butter

⅓ cup chopped shallots

1 pound ground skinless boneless duck breast

¼ pound duck liver, finely chopped by hand or in a food processor

1 cup cooked wild rice

1 cup whole wheat bread crumbs

¼ cup chopped parsley

2 tablespoons chopped fresh marjoram or 1½ teaspoons dried

2 teaspoons grated orange peel

1 teaspoon salt

1 teaspoon cracked black pepper

½ teaspoon ground mace

¼ teaspoon ground cloves

2 eggs

In a small glass bowl or a saucepan, combine the cherries, apricots, Madeira, and vinegar. Cover and bring just to a simmer in a microwave oven or on the stovetop. Remove from the heat and let stand 15 minutes until fruit is softened and plumped. In a small skillet, heat the butter and cook the shallots over medium heat, stirring often, until just softened, about 2 minutes.

Preheat the oven to 350 degrees. In a large mixing bowl, use your hands to gently but thoroughly combine the ground duck breast, liver, wild rice, bread crumbs, parsley, marjoram, orange peel, salt, pepper, mace, cloves, eggs, fruit and liquid, and cooked shallots.

In a 13 by 9-inch baking pan, shape the mixture into a 9 by 5-inch loaf, or pat it into a 9 by 5-inch loaf pan, smoothing the top.

Bake until the loaf is firm, the top is richly browned, and a meat thermometer inserted into the center of the loaf registers 160 degrees, about 1 hour. Let the meatloaf stand in the pan for 10 minutes before slicing to serve.

Turkey Club Squares

6 servings

*A*merica has invented many good food combinations, and the club sandwich is right up there on my list of favorites. So it's not surprising that I've translated it into meatloaf.

¼ pound smoked ham
6 slices bacon or turkey bacon
3 tablespoons mayonnaise, regular or low-fat
3 tablespoons Dijon mustard
1¼ pounds ground turkey
1 cup firm white bread crumbs
1 cup thinly sliced scallions

½ cup thawed, well-squeezed, and chopped frozen spinach
⅓ cup drained and chopped oil-packed sun-dried tomatoes
½ teaspoon salt
½ teaspoon freshly ground pepper
1 egg

Preheat the oven to 350 degrees. Cut the ham into chunks and finely chop them in a food processor. In a large skillet, partially cook the bacon until some of the fat is rendered. Remove the bacon from the skillet and reserve it. In a large mixing bowl, stir together the mayonnaise and mustard. Remove ¼ cup of the mixture to a small bowl and reserve it.

To the mustard mixture in the large bowl, add the ground turkey, bread crumbs, scallions, spinach, sun-dried tomatoes, salt, pepper, egg, and chopped ham. Use your hands to gently but thoroughly mix the meatloaf. Pat the mixture into a shallow 2-quart baking pan. Spread the top with the reserved ¼ cup mustard mixture, then lay the bacon slices over the mustard mixture.

Bake until the loaf is firm, the top is richly browned, and a meat thermometer inserted in the center of the loaf registers 160 degrees, 45 to 50 minutes. Let the meatloaf stand in the baking pan for 5 to 10 minutes before cutting into squares to serve.

Leftovers: Reheat chunks and serve warm on a bed of raw spinach tossed with a creamy buttermilk salad dressing and accompanied by white toast points.

Turkey Paprikash Squares

6 servings

*A*tender, juicy loaf that isn't too highly spiced, this one is good family fare. But if you increase the paprika and serve it with Two-Tomato Gravy (page 151), buttered poppy-seed noodles, and sautéed beet greens, it becomes a rustic Saturday night supper for friends.

1 tablespoon vegetable oil
1 onion, chopped
2 tablespoons sweet Hungarian
   paprika
1½ pounds ground turkey
1 cup whole wheat bread crumbs
1 cup seeded and diced plum
   tomatoes (2 or 3 tomatoes)
½ cup chopped flat-leaf parsley

6 tablespoons sour cream, regular
   or reduced-fat
2 tablespoons chopped fresh
   marjoram or 1½ teaspoons dried
1 teaspoon salt
½ teaspoon freshly ground pepper
½ teaspoon ground cumin
1 egg
⅓ cup chili sauce

Preheat the oven to 350 degrees. In a medium skillet, heat the oil and cook the onion, covered, over medium-low heat until softened, about 5 minutes. Uncover and raise the heat to medium-high. Cook the onion, stirring often, until it is deep golden and very fragrant, 4 to 7 minutes. Stir in the paprika and cook 1 minute more.

In a large mixing bowl, use your hands to gently but thoroughly combine the ground turkey, bread crumbs, tomatoes, parsley, 4 tablespoon of the sour cream, marjoram, salt, pepper, cumin, egg, and cooked onion. Pat the mixture into a shallow 2-quart baking pan. In a small dish, stir together the remaining 2 tablespoons sour cream and the chili sauce. Spread over the top of the loaf.

Bake until the loaf is firm and the top is richly browned, 45 to 50 minutes. Let the meatloaf stand in the pan for 5 to 10 minutes before cutting into squares to serve.

Leftovers: Serve cold squares as part of a lunch platter that includes coleslaw and pickled beets.

Turkey Picadillo Squares

6 servings

*P*icadillo is a spicy cooked ground-beef mixture of Cuban origin. The mix of savory, sweet, and peppery does great things for the neutral taste of ground turkey in this meatloaf. Serve it with a spinach salad tossed with orange segments and dressed with a tart citrus vinaigrette.

2 tablespoons olive oil
1 onion, chopped
1 red bell pepper
3 cloves garlic, minced
¼ cup dry red wine
1½ pounds ground turkey
1 cup firm fresh white bread crumbs
1 cup cooked white rice
1 can (4 ounces) chopped mild green chiles, drained

⅔ cup bottled chili sauce
⅓ cup coarsely chopped pitted green olives
¼ cup raisins
2 tablespoons rinsed and drained small capers
¼ teaspoon cayenne
1 egg
¼ cup sliced almonds

Preheat the oven to 350 degrees. In a medium skillet, heat the oil and cook the onion and bell pepper over medium heat, stirring often, until just softened, about 4 minutes. Add the garlic and cook for 1 minute. Add the wine and simmer until the liquid is nearly evaporated, about 3 minutes.

In a large mixing bowl, use your hands to gently but thoroughly combine the turkey, bread crumbs, rice, chiles, ⅓ cup of the chili sauce, olives, raisins, capers, cayenne, egg, and cooked vegetables.

Pat the mixture into a shallow 2-quart baking pan. Spread the remaining ⅓ cup chili sauce over the top. Sprinkle with the almonds.

Bake the loaf until it is firm and the top is richly browned, 45 to 50 minutes. Let the meatloaf stand in the pan for 5 to 10 minutes before cutting into squares to serve.

Leftovers: Make sandwiches with sliced or chunks of cold meatloaf in Cuban or hero rolls spread with a mixture of equal parts chili sauce and mayonnaise. Add some fresh spinach leaves to the sandwich.

Turkey and Jalapeño Corn Bread Squares

6 servings

*T*his is a great use for day-old corn bread or corn muffins and it is a really easy meatloaf supper that is nicely completed with little more than a big green salad and some warm tortillas.

1 tablespoon vegetable oil
1 onion, chopped
1 red bell pepper, chopped
2 tablespoons seeded and chopped
  fresh or pickled jalapeño peppers
  (about 2 jalapeños)
2 tablespoons chili powder

1½ pounds ground turkey
2 cups finely crumbled day-old
  corn bread or corn muffins
¾ teaspoon salt
2 eggs
¾ cup prepared salsa

Preheat the oven to 350 degrees. In a medium skillet, heat the oil and cook the onion and bell pepper over medium heat, stirring often, until just softened, about 4 minutes. Add the jalapeño and chili powder and cook, stirring, for 1 minute.

In a large mixing bowl, use your hands to gently but thoroughly combine the turkey, corn bread, salt, eggs, and cooked vegetables.

Pat the mixture into a shallow 2-quart baking pan. Spread the salsa over the top.

Bake until the loaf is firm and the top is richly browned, 45 to 50 minutes. Let the meatloaf stand in the baking pan for 5 to 10 minutes before serving.

Leftovers: Cut into small pieces, reheat, and serve in taco shells garnished with shredded lettuce, shredded Jack cheese, and more salsa.

Chicken Pot Pie Loaf

6 servings

*A*ll the flavors of chicken pot pie, and even a pastry crust! This loaf is particularly good with Herbed Chicken Gravy (page 149), but it is really moist and juicy enough to stand on its own.

2 eggs
1½ pounds ground chicken
1 cup coarsely crushed dry
   herb-seasoned bread stuffing
   mix
1 cup diced cooked waxy potato
   (about 1 large potato)
1 cup cooked small pearl
   onions

1 cup frozen peas and carrots,
   thawed
3 tablespoons dry sherry
1 teaspoon salt
½ teaspoon freshly ground pepper
½ teaspoon ground celery seed
Pastry for a single-crust 9-inch pie
   or 1 disk from a 14-ounce
   package refrigerated piecrusts

Preheat the oven to 400 degrees. In a large mixing bowl, whisk the eggs. Remove 1 tablespoon beaten egg to a small dish and reserve to use as a pastry glaze. Add the chicken, stuffing mix, potato, onions, peas and carrots, sherry, salt, pepper, and celery seed to the remaining egg in the mixing bowl. Use your hands to gently but thoroughly mix the meatloaf.

Pat the meatloaf into a 10-inch pie plate. If using homemade pie pastry, roll on a lightly floured surface to an 11-inch round. Place the homemade pastry or store-bought pastry disk on top of the meatloaf, crimping the edges against the rim of the dish. Use a small knife to make several slits in the pastry, then brush the pastry with the reserved beaten egg.

Bake the meatloaf for 30 minutes, then reduce the heat to 350 degrees and bake an additional 10 to 15 minutes until the pastry is rich golden. Let the meatloaf stand in the pan for 10 minutes before cutting into wedges to serve.

Sesame Chicken Squares

6 servings

*T*his meatloaf is inspired by the wonderful rich taste of sesame noodles, a popular Chinese restaurant dish. You can buy toasted sesame seeds in the Asian section of the market or you can easily toast your own by tossing them in a dry skillet set over medium heat just until they are golden and fragrant. To prevent overcooking, immediately transfer the seeds from the skillet to a plate to cool.

*2 teaspoons dark or toasted
  sesame oil*
3 cloves garlic, minced
1½ pounds ground chicken
1 cup cooked white rice
1 cup firm white bread crumbs
1 cup thinly sliced scallions
¼ cup chopped cilantro

*½ cup coarsely chopped roasted
  peanuts*
3 tablespoons toasted sesame seeds
2 tablespoons peanut butter
2 tablespoons soy sauce
2 tablespoons hoisin sauce
½ teaspoon freshly ground pepper
1 egg

Preheat the oven to 350 degrees. In a small skillet, heat the sesame oil and cook the garlic over medium-low heat, stirring constantly for 1 minute. In a large mixing bowl, use your hands to gently but thoroughly combine the ground chicken, rice, bread crumbs, scallions, cilantro, ¼ cup of the chopped peanuts, sesame seeds, peanut butter, soy sauce, hoisin sauce, pepper, egg, and cooked garlic mixture.

Pat the mixture into a shallow 2-quart baking pan. Sprinkle the top with the remaining ¼ cup chopped peanuts.

Bake until the loaf is firm and the top is richly browned, 45 to 50 minutes. Let the meatloaf stand in the pan for 5 to 10 minutes before cutting into squares to serve.

Leftovers: Serve reheated or at room temperature on vermicelli tossed with soy sauce, sesame oil, a spoonful of peanut butter, and a sprinkling of sesame seeds.

Cajun Grilled Turkey Loaves

6 servings

*T*hough I've never been fond of the burnt crust on Cajun "blackened" foods, I do like all the spices and herbs that go into blackening seasoning. With a meatloaf, they can be mixed into the meat and the result is juicy flavor throughout and just a hint of charring on the outside.

1½ tablespoons vegetable oil
1 onion, chopped
1 celery rib, chopped
2 cloves garlic, minced
1½ pounds ground turkey
1 cup firm white bread crumbs
2 teaspoons paprika

2 teaspoons chili powder
1½ teaspoons dried oregano
1 teaspoon dried thyme
½ teaspoon ground cumin
½ teaspoon salt
¼ teaspoon cayenne
1 egg

Prepare a medium-hot barbecue fire or preheat a gas grill. Coat the grill rack with vegetable oil or nonstick vegetable spray. In a medium skillet, heat the oil and cook the onion and celery over medium heat, stirring often, until just softened, about 4 minutes. Add the garlic and cook 1 minute.

In a large mixing bowl, use your hands to gently but thoroughly combine the turkey, bread crumbs, paprika, chili powder, oregano, thyme, cumin, salt, cayenne, egg, and cooked vegetables.

Divide the mixture into 6 parts and form each into an oval loaf about 1 inch thick. Grill on one side for 10 minutes. Turn with a spatula and grill until the meatloaves are cooked through and juices run clear, 10 to 15 minutes longer.

Leftovers: Reheat chunks by simmering in Cajun-style stewed tomatoes, then ladle over plain rice or pasta.

Grilled Tuscan Turkey Loaves

6 servings

*T*here are endless themes for classic bruschetta, but I'll bet this is the first meatloaf variation. My very traditional Italian relatives have given this recipe a stamp of approval, and that is no small event among these folks. So you can feel confident cooking it for your Italian relatives or friends, too.

6 tablespoons extra-virgin olive oil
6 cloves garlic, minced
1½ cups seeded and chopped ripe
  tomatoes (about 3 tomatoes)
1½ pounds ground turkey
1 cup finely chopped red onion
1 cup Italian bread crumbs
½ cup chopped basil

2 tablespoons balsamic vinegar
1 teaspoon salt
½ teaspoon freshly ground pepper
½ teaspoon crushed hot pepper
  flakes
1 egg
6 slices Italian bread
Basil sprigs for garnish

Prepare a medium-hot barbecue fire or preheat a gas grill. Coat the grill rack with vegetable oil or nonstick vegetable spray.

In a small bowl, combine the oil and garlic. Let stand 15 minutes. Place tomatoes in a mixing bowl and add about 2 tablespoons of the garlic oil. Stir and then let the tomatoes marinate while grilling the meatloaves. In another mixing bowl, combine the turkey, onion, bread crumbs, chopped basil, balsamic vinegar, salt, pepper, pepper flakes, and egg.

Divide the mixture into 6 parts and form each into an oval loaf about 1 inch thick. Grill on one side for 10 minutes. Turn with a spatula and grill until the meatloaves are cooked through and juices run clear, 10 to 15 minutes longer.

A few minutes before the meatloaves are done, lightly grill both sides of the Italian bread, then brush one side with the reserved garlic oil.

Serve the meatloaves on the grilled toast with the diced tomatoes spooned on top. Garnish with the basil sprigs.

Grilled Dill Turkey Loaves

6 servings

*D*ill and mustard take nicely to grilling. These are simple and sophisticated loaves that are particularly good served on grilled whole wheat Italian bread slices with grilled tomato slices and a sprig of dill as garnish—another variation on bruschetta.

1½ pounds ground turkey
1 cup whole wheat bread crumbs
1 cup thinly sliced scallions
¼ cup chopped fresh dill
1½ tablespoons grainy Dijon
 mustard

1 tablespoon mayonnaise, regular
 or low-fat
½ teaspoon salt
½ teaspoon freshly ground
 pepper
1 egg

Prepare a medium-hot barbecue fire or preheat a gas grill. Coat the grill rack with vegetable oil or nonstick vegetable spray. In a large mixing bowl, use your hands to gently but thoroughly combine all of the ingredients.

Divide the mixture into 6 parts and form each into an oval loaf about 1 inch thick. Grill on one side for 10 minutes. Turn with a spatula and grill until the meatloaves are cooked through and juices run clear, 10 to 15 minutes longer.

Leftovers: Slice the meatloaves and serve cold in sandwiches with sliced tomatoes on whole wheat bread spread with mustard and mayonnaise.

Lebanese Grilled Chicken Loaves

6 servings

*G*rilling is a favored way of cooking throughout the Mediterranean. The heady herbs and spices of the region take well to the toasting that an open fire produces. These are wonderful as part of a summer supper that includes a couscous salad on a bed of romaine lettuce leaves, grilled pita breads, and lush apricots for dessert.

1/3 cup chopped fresh mint
2/3 cup plain yogurt
1 1/2 pounds ground chicken
1 cup whole wheat bread crumbs
2/3 cup chopped red onion
1 1/2 teaspoons ground cumin

1 teaspoon salt
1/2 teaspoon freshly ground
pepper
1/2 teaspoon ground coriander
1/4 teaspoon cayenne
1 egg

Prepare a medium-hot barbecue fire or preheat a gas grill. Coat the grill rack with vegetable oil or nonstick vegetable spray. In a large mixing bowl, stir together the mint and yogurt. Remove 1/2 cup of the mixture to a small bowl and reserve to brush on the meatloaves.

To the yogurt mixture in the large bowl, add the chicken, bread crumbs, onion, cumin, salt, pepper, coriander, cayenne, and egg.

Divide the mixture into 6 parts and form each into an oval loaf about 1 inch thick. Brush both sides with the remaining yogurt mixture. Grill on one side for 10 minutes. Turn with a spatula and grill until the meatloaves are cooked through and the juices run clear, 10 to 15 minutes longer.

Leftovers: Cut into chunks and serve at room temperature stuffed into pita breads garnished with a dollop of yogurt, chopped mint, and red onion.

Barbecued Chicken Loaves

6 servings

*T*will grill most anything, and meatloaves have become a particular passion. Barbecued meatloaf has a crusty edge and a juicy, seasoned interior, like a good burger but better. This chicken loaf is the easiest barbecued loaf in my repertoire.

1 tablespoon vegetable oil
1 onion, chopped
1 celery rib, chopped
1½ pounds ground chicken

1½ cups dry corn bread stuffing mix
¾ cup prepared thick barbecue sauce
1 teaspoon hot pepper sauce
1 egg

Prepare a medium-hot barbecue fire or preheat a gas grill. Coat the grill rack with vegetable oil or nonstick vegetable spray. In a medium skillet, heat the oil and cook the onion and celery over medium heat, stirring often, until the vegetables are softened, about 5 minutes.

In a large mixing bowl, use your hands to gently but thoroughly combine the chicken, 1 cup of the stuffing mix, ¼ cup of the barbecue sauce, hot pepper sauce, egg, and cooked vegetables.

Divide the mixture into 6 parts and form each into an oval loaf about 1 inch thick. Spread the remaining stuffing mix on a plate and dip the loaves into the stuffing to coat lightly. Grill the loaves on one side for 10 minutes. Turn with a spatula, brush the cooked side of the loaves with the remaining ½ cup barbecue sauce, then grill until the meatloaves are cooked through and the juices run clear, 10 to 15 minutes longer.

Leftovers: Reheat chunks in bottled barbecue sauce thinned with beer. Ladle chunks and sauce into sandwich rolls along with coleslaw for a hot barbecue sandwich.

Curried Chicken and Apple Loaves

6 servings

*T*hese loaves are particularly tasty when grilled, but they can also be baked as individual loaves in a 350-degree oven for about 30 minutes or in a traditional 9 by 5-inch loaf pan for about an hour.

1 tablespoon vegetable oil
1 onion, chopped
1 tart apple, peeled, cored, and coarsely chopped
2 teaspoons curry powder
1 teaspoon ground cardamom
1½ pounds ground chicken

1 cup whole wheat bread crumbs
½ cup chopped prepared mango chutney
1 teaspoon salt
¼ teaspoon cayenne
1 egg
½ cup plain yogurt

Prepare a medium-hot barbecue fire or preheat a gas grill. In a medium skillet, heat the oil and cook the onion and apple over medium heat, stirring often, until the onion is just softened, about 4 minutes. Stir in the curry powder and cardamom and cook for 1 minute more.

In a large mixing bowl, use your hands to gently but thoroughly combine the chicken, bread crumbs, ¼ cup of the chutney, salt, cayenne, egg, and cooked onion mixture. Divide into 6 portions and form each into an individual oval loaf, about ¾ inch thick. In a small bowl, stir together the remaining chutney and yogurt.

Grill, turning once or twice, until the loaves are cooked through, with no traces of pink, 15 to 18 minutes total. Serve the loaves dolloped with the chutney-yogurt.

Seafood Loaves

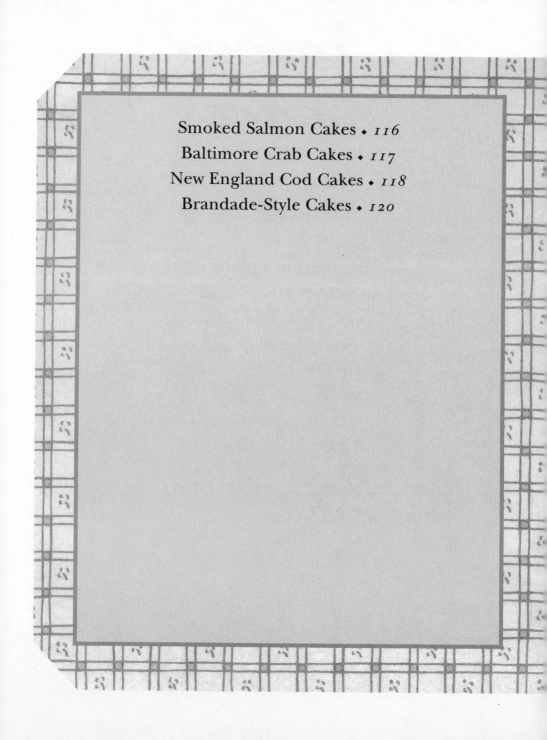

Seafood Loaves

Seafood has long been held in high esteem as the key to velvety-textured, creamy-rich terrines and mousselike loaves. The classic combination of scallops and sole has a delicate flavor and ivory color that is a lovely background for bits of golden carrots, ruby-red peppers, or verdant asparagus. Salmon produces a startlingly beautiful shell-pink loaf with a sturdier texture and more pronounced flavor that holds up wonderfully to assertive herbs and vegetable layering.

With a little imagination, a seafood loaf can capture the essence of all sorts of traditional seafood dishes. Rice is the starch in Seafood Paella Loaf and a good bread forms the basis for Southwest Tuna Melt Loaf. Baltimore Crab Cakes and New England Cod Cakes are plump patties or miniloaves whose popularity goes way beyond their namesake geographical boundaries.

Like meat and poultry, the best seafood is the freshest. Shrimp, which is almost always shipped to market frozen, is the exception and when properly frozen and thawed is nearly indistinguishable from its fresh counterpart.

Because seafood has more natural moisture and a softer texture than meat or poultry, these recipes usually contain more breading and less liquid. Though fish and shellfish are not universally interchangeable in recipes, you can often substitute within similar categories, such as catfish for cod or swordfish for salmon, and achieve equally good results.

Dilled Salmon Loaf

6 servings

*S*ome fish markets are now offering ground salmon, which can be a great convenience (although it isn't hard to grind it yourself in a food processor). As always, in order to ensure freshness and quality, buy seafood from a purveyor whom you know and trust. This is one of the simplest seafood loaves in my repertoire, which is probably why it is made so often at my house.

1½ pounds skinless, boneless salmon fillet, cut into chunks (or use fresh ground salmon)
1½ cups firm white bread crumbs
1 cup chopped red onion
¼ cup chopped fresh dill
2 tablespoons Dijon mustard

2 tablespoons lemon juice
¾ teaspoon freshly ground pepper
½ teaspoon salt
2 eggs
Dill sprigs and lemon wedges for garnish
¾ cup Lemon-Caper Sour Cream (page 156)

Preheat the oven to 350 degrees. Butter a 9 by 5-inch loaf pan or coat with nonstick vegetable spray. In a food processor, pulse to finely chop the salmon. Transfer to a mixing bowl and add the bread crumbs, onion, dill, mustard, lemon juice, pepper, salt, and eggs. Use your hands to gently but thoroughly combine the ingredients.

Pat the mixture into the prepared pan. Bake until the loaf is firm and crusty on top and a meat thermometer inserted into the center of the loaf registers 155 degrees, about 1 hour. Let the loaf stand in the pan for at least 10 minutes before slicing to serve garnished with dill sprigs and lemon wedges. Serve with Lemon-Caper Sour Cream.

Leftovers: Serve cold, cut into chunks, on a bed of pasta that has been tossed with additional chopped dill and Lemon-Caper Sour Cream thinned with a little milk.

Salmon and Spinach Croquette Loaf

6 servings

*A*lthough cooked fresh salmon is wonderful, canned salmon works just as well, and it is cheaper and always available. Firm-textured, like a meatloaf, this will become a family favorite.

1 tablespoon unsalted butter
1 onion, finely chopped
1 celery rib, finely chopped
¼ cup chopped flat-leaf parsley
1 package (10 ounces) frozen chopped spinach, thawed and squeezed of all excess moisture
1 pound cooked fresh skinless, boneless salmon or 1 can (15½ ounces) salmon, drained, skin and bones removed
1 cup unseasoned dry bread crumbs

¼ cup mayonnaise, regular or reduced-fat
1 tablespoon lemon juice
1 teaspoon grated lemon peel
1 teaspoon grated orange peel
1 teaspoon hot pepper sauce
½ teaspoon ground allspice
½ teaspoon salt
½ teaspoon freshly ground pepper
¼ teaspoon ground mace
1 egg
Lemon wedges for garnish

Preheat the oven to 350 degrees. Butter a 9 by 5-inch loaf pan or coat with nonstick vegetable spray. In a medium skillet, heat the butter over medium heat and cook the onion and celery, stirring often, until softened, about 5 minutes. Add the parsley and spinach. Cook, stirring, for 1 minute.

In a large mixing bowl, use your fingers to flake the salmon. Add the bread crumbs, mayonnaise, lemon juice, lemon and orange peels, hot pepper sauce, allspice, salt, pepper, mace, egg, and cooked vegetables. Use your hands to gently but thoroughly combine the ingredients.

Pat the mixture into the prepared loaf pan. Bake until the loaf is firm and crusty on top, about 1 hour. Let the loaf stand in the pan for at least 10 minutes before slicing to serve garnished with lemon wedges.

Leftovers: Make sandwiches with whole wheat bread, mayonnaise flavored with lemon, and soft lettuce leaves.

Herbed Scallop and Sole Terrine

6 servings

*S*erve this springtime green and white terrine warm or cold—it is equally good either way.

1 tablespoon butter
1 cup packed watercress sprigs
1 cup thinly sliced scallions
2 tablespoons chopped fresh
   tarragon or 1½ teaspoons dried
1 pound fillet of sole, cut
   into chunks
½ pound sea or bay scallops
2 eggs
1½ cups firm white bread crumbs

3 tablespoons lemon juice
1 teaspoon grated lemon
   peel
1 teaspoon dry mustard
1 teaspoon salt
½ teaspoon white pepper
⅛ teaspoon grated nutmeg
1½ cups chilled heavy cream
Lemon wedges and watercress
   sprigs for garnish

Preheat the oven to 350 degrees. Butter a 9 by 5-inch loaf pan. In a medium skillet, heat the butter and cook the watercress and scallions, stirring often over medium heat, until the vegetables are wilted, 3 to 5 minutes. Remove from the heat, stir in the tarragon, and let cool.

In a food processor, finely chop together the sole and scallops. Add the eggs, bread crumbs, lemon juice and peel, mustard, salt, pepper, and nutmeg. Process to blend well. With the motor running, pour the cream through the feed tube and process until blended and thick, about 10 seconds. Transfer about two-thirds of the mixture to a bowl. Add the wilted watercress mixture to the remaining one-third of the fish mixture and process just to blend well.

In the prepared loaf pan, spread about half of the plain seafood mixture evenly over the bottom. Dollop all of the green mixture over the plain seafood layer in the pan and use a metal spatula to carefully spread it over the top. Dollop the remaining plain seafood mixture over the green mixture and carefully spread to cover.

Set the pan in a larger pan half-filled with hot water. Bake until firm to the touch and an instant-read thermometer inserted into the center registers 155 degrees, 1 to 1¼ hours.

Let the loaf stand in the pan for at least 20 minutes before slicing.

Pink Seafood Mousse Loaf

6 servings

*T*his airy, yet rich pink seafood mousse looks and tastes terrific warm or cold. Served warm, the mousse is fluffy and light, while chilling compacts the loaf for a more dense and creamy texture. Both are delicious.

*1 pound medium or small peeled
  and deveined shrimp*
*⅔ pound skinless, boneless salmon
  fillet, cut into chunks*
2 eggs
½ cup firm white bread crumbs
2 tablespoons tomato paste

1 tablespoon lemon juice
1 teaspoon paprika
1 teaspoon salt
½ teaspoon white pepper
*1 cup chilled heavy
  cream*
1 cup chopped scallions

Preheat the oven to 350 degrees. Butter a 9 by 5-inch loaf pan. Coarsely chop ½ pound of the shrimp and reserve. In a food processor, finely chop together the salmon and the remaining ½ pound of shrimp. Add the eggs, bread crumbs, tomato paste, lemon juice, paprika, salt, and pepper. Process briefly to blend. With the motor running, pour the cream through the feed tube and process just until blended and thick, about 10 seconds. Add the scallions and chopped shrimp, and pulse the machine four or five times just until evenly distributed.

Scrape the mixture into the prepared loaf pan. Set the pan in a larger pan half-filled with hot water. Bake until the mousse is firm to the touch and an instant-read thermometer inserted into the center of the loaf registers 155 degrees, 1 to 1¼ hours.

Let the loaf stand in the pan for at least 20 minutes before slicing to serve.

Leftovers: Serve cold on a bed of young spinach leaves topped with a spoonful of diced tomatoes dressed with a little olive oil and lemon juice.

Shrimp and Crab Loaf

6 servings

*T*he fabulous crab cake at Susanna Foo's spectacular restaurant in Philadelphia is the inspiration for this seafood loaf. Like all of Susanna's food, the juxtaposition of flavors and textures is brilliant.

8 slices firm white bread, toasted
1 tablespoon butter
1 pound medium or small peeled
* and deveined shrimp*
¼ cup heavy cream
2 tablespoons lemon juice
1 tablespoon gin
1 tablespoon soy sauce
1 tablespoon finely chopped
* fresh ginger*
½ teaspoon freshly ground
* pepper*
2 eggs
1 cup thinly sliced scallions
½ cup drained and coarsely
* chopped canned water*
* chestnuts*
⅓ cup chopped cilantro
½ pound fresh lump crabmeat,
* picked over*

Preheat the oven to 350 degrees. Butter a shallow 2-quart baking dish or coat with nonstick vegetable spray. In a food processor, make crumbs of the toasted bread. Measure 1½ cups of the crumbs into a mixing bowl. Heat the butter in a small skillet and toss the remaining crumbs to moisten. Set aside for the topping. Coarsely chop ½ pound of the shrimp. Set aside.

In a food processor, puree the remaining ½ pound of the shrimp with the cream, lemon juice, gin, soy sauce, ginger, and pepper. Add the eggs and process to blend. Transfer the mixture to the mixing bowl with the bread crumbs. Add the scallions, water chestnuts, and cilantro. Use your hands or a spoon to blend. Add the chopped shrimp to the mixing bowl along with the crabmeat. Use your hands or a spoon to gently but thoroughly blend in.

Pat the mixture into the prepared pan and sprinkle the top with the buttered crumbs. Bake until the loaf is firm and browned, 40 to 45 minutes. Let the loaf stand in the pan for 5 to 10 minutes before cutting into squares to serve.

Everybody Loves Meatloaf

Casino Clam Loaf

6 servings

*C*lams casino has been a familiar appetizer on restaurant menus since the 1950s. Their popularity stems from the unbeatable combination of briny clams, smoky bacon, sweet peppers, and piquant seasoned bread crumbs. I thought that the whole thing could move into a loaf form, and here is the tasty result of my experiment.

6 slices bacon
1 onion, chopped
1 red bell pepper, chopped
3 cloves garlic, minced
2 cups firm white or Italian
*   bread crumbs*
2 cups coarsely chopped clams,
*   fresh or canned, drained*
¼ cup grated Parmesan cheese
¼ cup chopped flat-leaf parsley
3 tablespoons chopped fresh basil

1 tablespoon chopped fresh oregano
*   or 1 teaspoon dried*
1 tablespoon chopped fresh
*   marjoram or 1 teaspoon dried*
¼ teaspoon salt
¼ teaspoon freshly ground pepper
¼ teaspoon dried hot pepper flakes
2 tablespoons Pernod or other
*   anise liqueur*
1 tablespoon fresh lemon juice
2 eggs

Preheat the oven to 350 degrees. In a large skillet, cook the bacon over medium heat until limp and about 1 tablespoon of fat is rendered, about 5 minutes. Remove the bacon from the skillet and reserve. Add the onion and bell pepper to the skillet. Cook, stirring often, until the vegetables are just softened, about 4 minutes. Add the garlic and cook for 1 minute.

In a large mixing bowl, use your hands to gently but thoroughly combine the bread crumbs, clams, cheese, parsley, basil, oregano, marjoram, salt, pepper, pepper flakes, liqueur, lemon juice, eggs, and cooked vegetables.

Pat the mixture into a shallow 2-quart baking pan. Arrange the partially cooked bacon on top. Bake until the loaf is firm, the bacon is crisp, and the top is crusty, about 45 minutes. Let stand 5 to 10 minutes in the pan before cutting into squares to serve.

Leftovers: Serve cold with a lemon wedge and sliced tomatoes.

Shrimp Fried Rice Loaf

6 servings

*T*his is another case of gilding the lily. Fried rice is fine, but I like the ingredients even better fashioned into a loaf. It gets a wonderfully crusty top and it's good cold, too. Best of all, it's yet another idea for using up the leftover rice that always seems to be present in my refrigerator.

1 tablespoon vegetable oil
1 red bell pepper, chopped
1 tablespoon sesame oil
1 cup thinly sliced scallions
2 cloves garlic, minced
1 tablespoon minced fresh ginger
2 teaspoons minced jalapeño pepper
1 tablespoon nam pla (Thai fish sauce)

1 tablespoon reduced-sodium soy sauce
1 tablespoon lime juice
½ teaspoon grated lime peel
3 eggs
3 cups cooked white rice
¾ cup firm white bread crumbs
½ pound cooked small or medium shrimp, diced
¼ cup chopped cilantro

Preheat the oven to 350 degrees. Coat a shallow 2-quart baking pan with nonstick vegetable spray. In a large skillet, heat the vegetable oil and cook the bell pepper, stirring occasionally, until just softened, about 3 minutes. Add the sesame oil, scallions, garlic, ginger, and jalapeño pepper. Cook, stirring, for 1 minute. Stir in the fish sauce, soy sauce, lime juice, and lime peel.

In a large mixing bowl, whisk the eggs, then add the rice, bread crumbs, and cooked vegetable mixture. Use your hands or a spoon to blend the ingredients together. Blend in the shrimp and cilantro.

Spoon the mixture into the prepared baking pan. Bake until the top is browned and crusty, 35 to 45 minutes. Let the loaf stand in the pan for at least 10 minutes before cutting into squares to serve. Serve warm or cold.

Seafood Paella Loaf

6 servings

*B*ecause I like it just as well cold for breakfast as hot for dinner, I always make more paella than we need for one meal. This crusty-edged loaf is a tasty result of an experiment with these planned leftovers. If saffron is too pricey for your budget, turmeric will give the same golden color. The Meatloaf Marinara Sauce (page 153) is a most complementary sauce, but the loaf is delicious without it, too.

½ pound chorizo or hot Italian sausage

1 small red bell pepper, coarsely chopped

1 small yellow bell pepper, coarsely chopped

1 onion, chopped

2 cloves garlic, minced

¼ teaspoon crushed saffron threads or turmeric

1 pound medium or small peeled and deveined shrimp, coarsely chopped

1 can (3½ ounces) smoked mussels, drained

2 cups cooked white rice

1 cup Italian bread crumbs

½ cup chopped flat-leaf parsley

¼ cup sliced or chopped green or black olives

2 tablespoons lemon juice

½ teaspoon ground cumin

½ teaspoon cayenne

¼ teaspoon salt

2 eggs

Preheat the oven to 350 degrees. Remove the sausage from its casing and crumble the meat into a large skillet. Cook the sausage over medium-high heat, stirring occasionally, until lightly browned, about 5 minutes. Drain off most of the excess fat. Add the red and yellow bell peppers and the onion to the skillet. Reduce the heat to medium and cook, stirring occasionally, until the vegetables are softened, about 5 minutes. Stir in the garlic and saffron and cook for 1 minute, stirring constantly.

In a large mixing bowl, use your hands to gently but thoroughly combine the shrimp, mussels, rice, bread crumbs, parsley, olives, lemon juice, cumin, cayenne, salt, eggs, and cooked sausage and vegetables.

Pat the mixture into a shallow 2-quart baking pan. Bake until the loaf is browned and the top is crusty, 40 to 45 minutes. Let the loaf stand in the pan for at least 10 minutes before cutting into squares to serve.

Southwest Tuna Melt Loaf

6 servings

*T*his is a bread pudding that cuts like a loaf. You can assemble it ahead, but serve it hot from the oven when it is still prettily puffed.

1½ tablespoons softened butter
8 slices firm white bread
1 can (12 ounces) solid white tuna
in water, drained and flaked
1½ cups milk
3 eggs

2 teaspoons Worcestershire sauce
1 teaspoon hot pepper sauce
1 teaspoon dry mustard
1½ cups grated Monterey Jack
cheese with hot peppers
⅓ cup diced pimiento

Preheat the oven to 350 degrees. Use about ½ tablespoon of the butter to grease a shallow 2-quart baking pan. Spread the remaining butter on both sides of the bread, then break the bread into large chunks and place in a single layer, close together, in the baking pan. Sprinkle the tuna over the bread.

In a mixing bowl, whisk together the milk, eggs, Worcestershire and hot pepper sauces, and mustard. Stir in the cheese and pimiento. Pour the mixture over the bread and tuna, pushing the bread slices into the liquid to absorb it.

Bake until the loaf is puffed and golden, 35 to 45 minutes. Serve immediately.

Everybody Loves Meatloaf

Clam Hash Cakes

6 servings

*H*ash is an American classic, and hash cakes are a miniature and more manageable version of the usual hash in a skillet. They also qualify quite nicely for inclusion in this chapter on seafood loaves.

¼ pound thick-cut bacon
1 pound diced cooked potatoes
  (about 3 cups)
2 cups coarsely chopped clams,
  fresh or canned, drained
2 cups firm white bread crumbs
1 cup thinly sliced scallions
3 tablespoons heavy cream
3 tablespoons chopped
  flat-leaf parsley

2 tablespoons chopped fresh thyme
  or 2 teaspoons dried
1 tablespoon chopped fresh oregano
  or 1 teaspoon dried
1 teaspoon hot pepper sauce
¼ teaspoon freshly ground pepper
2 eggs
2 tablespoons vegetable oil
Tangy Seafood Sauce (page 157),
  optional

In a large skillet over medium heat, cook the bacon until it is crisp and the fat is rendered, about 5 to 7 minutes. Using a slotted spoon, remove the bacon from the skillet, drain on paper towels, then crumble and reserve it. Pour off all but 2 tablespoons drippings from the skillet.

In a large mixing bowl, use your hands to gently but thoroughly combine the potatoes, clams, bread crumbs, scallions, cream, parsley, thyme, oregano, hot pepper sauce, pepper, eggs, and bacon. Divide the mixture into 6 parts, forming each into a patty about 3 inches in diameter. (The patties will seem loosely formed, but they will cook well.)

In the skillet used to cook the bacon, heat the drippings and the vegetable oil. Cook the hash cakes until the bottom is browned and crisp, 5 to 7 minutes. Use a spatula to carefully turn the patties and cook until the other side is browned and crisp, 5 to 7 minutes more.

Serve the hash cakes with the Tangy Seafood Sauce, if desired.

Smoked Salmon Cakes

6 servings

*A*small amount of good smoked salmon can add a lot of flavor when combined with fresh salmon. Since it will be chopped up anyway, ask for the end pieces and trimmings, which are usually far less expensive than perfect slices. These sophisticated fish cakes are especially good with Tarragon Tartar Sauce (page 157), accompanied by steamed asparagus and sautéed cherry tomatoes. It is a main course worthy of your finest company.

2½ cups firm white bread crumbs
½ cup chopped flat-leaf parsley
2 tablespoons unsalted butter
1 onion, finely chopped
½ red bell pepper, finely chopped
¾ pound skinless fresh salmon fillet,
  cut into chunks

¼ pound smoked salmon, cut
  into chunks
2 teaspoons Dijon mustard
1 teaspoon Worcestershire sauce
1 teaspoon hot pepper sauce
2 eggs
2 tablespoons vegetable oil

In a large mixing bowl, combine the bread crumbs and the parsley. Transfer about 1 cup of the mixture to a plate and reserve for dredging the cakes. In a large skillet, heat 1 tablespoon of the butter and cook the onion and bell pepper over medium heat, stirring often, until the vegetables are softened, about 5 minutes. Transfer to the mixing bowl. In a food processor, pulse to coarsely chop the fresh and smoked salmon together. Add to the mixing bowl along with the mustard, Worcestershire, hot pepper sauce, and the eggs. Use your hands to gently but thoroughly combine the ingredients.

Divide the mixture into 6 parts, forming each into a patty about 3 inches in diameter. Dredge the patties in the reserved bread crumbs to coat both sides. Place in a single layer on a baking sheet and refrigerate for at least 20 minutes or up to 4 hours.

In a large skillet, heat the remaining 1 tablespoon butter and the oil. Cook the fish cakes over medium heat until the bottom is crisp and dark golden, about 5 minutes. Use a spatula to carefully turn the cakes and cook until the other side is dark golden, about 5 minutes more.

Serve the fish cakes with the Tarragon Tartar Sauce, if desired.

Everybody Loves Meatloaf

Baltimore Crab Cakes

6 servings

*M*y son, a Baltimore resident and crab-cake connoisseur, says that these are the ultimate seafood loaves. Fish cakes contain all the basic "loaf" elements, including bread crumbs and eggs. So with pleasure I'm including these crab cakes in the expanded repertoire of seafood loaves. The Tarragon Tartar Sauce (page 157) is a breeze to make, but you could use a good brand of bottled tartar sauce, too.

2½ cups firm white bread crumbs

⅓ cup thinly sliced scallions

2 tablespoons mayonnaise, regular or low-fat

2 teaspoons lemon juice

1 teaspoon Worcestershire sauce

1 teaspoon Old Bay or other Maryland-style seafood seasoning mix

1 teaspoon dry mustard

¼ teaspoon cayenne

2 eggs

1 pound lump crabmeat, drained and picked over

4 tablespoons vegetable oil

In a large mixing bowl, use your hands to gently but thoroughly combine 1½ cups of the bread crumbs, the scallions, mayonnaise, lemon juice, Worcestershire sauce, seafood seasoning, mustard, cayenne, and eggs. Add the crabmeat and mix gently to blend in without breaking up the pieces of crab too much.

Divide the mixture into 6 parts, forming each into a large patty about 3 inches in diameter. Place the remaining 1 cup of bread crumbs on a plate and dip each patty into the crumbs to coat both sides. Place the patties in a single layer on a baking sheet. Refrigerate at least 20 minutes or up to 4 hours.

Heat the oil in a large skillet and cook the patties over medium heat until the bottom is crisp and dark golden, about 5 minutes. Turn carefully with a spatula and cook until the other side is crisp and dark golden, about 5 minutes more.

Serve the crab cakes with the Tarragon Tartar Sauce, if desired.

New England Cod Cakes

6 servings

*F*ish chowder and cod cakes are standard fare in coastal New England, where I live. Both are generally seasoned with thyme, parsley, and bacon or salt pork. Cod cakes, unlike other fish cakes, often contain mashed potatoes. Who am I to tinker with Yankee tradition?

1 pound cod fillets
1 cup milk
¼ cup bottled clam juice
1 pound all-purpose potatoes,
*   peeled and cut into 2-inch chunks*
*   (see Note)*
1 tablespoon butter
6 slices bacon
1 onion, finely chopped
½ cup chopped flat-leaf parsley,
*   plus 6 sprigs for garnish*

2 tablespoons chopped fresh
*   thyme or 1½ teaspoons*
*   dried*
½ teaspoon freshly ground
*   pepper*
¼ teaspoon salt
1 egg
¼ cup all-purpose flour
2 tablespoons vegetable oil
Lemon wedges and parsley sprigs
*   for garnish*

In a medium saucepan, gently simmer the cod in the milk and clam juice, covered, over medium-low heat, until the fish is opaque, about 4 minutes. Using a slotted spoon, transfer the fish to a large mixing bowl. (The fish may be falling apart.) Reserve the poaching liquid.

Cook the potatoes in boiling salted water to cover until very tender, about 20 minutes. Drain well and mash with the butter and 2 to 4 tablespoons of the poaching liquid to make stiff mashed potatoes. Add the potatoes to the mixing bowl with the fish.

In a large skillet, cook the bacon over medium heat until crisp, about 5 to 7 minutes. Drain the bacon on paper towels, then crumble it. Pour off all but 1 tablespoon of drippings, then cook the onion in the drippings over medium heat, stirring until softened, about 5 minutes. Add the bacon and onion to the cod mixture along with the chopped parsley, thyme, pepper, salt, and egg. Use your hands to gently but thoroughly combine the ingredients.

Divide the mixture into 6 parts and form each into a patty between 3 and 4 inches in diameter. Place the flour on a plate and dredge the patties to coat both sides. Place the patties in a single layer on a baking sheet. Refrigerate at least 20 minutes or up to 4 hours.

In a large skillet, heat the oil and cook the patties until the bottom is browned and crisp, 5 to 7 minutes. Use a spatula to carefully turn the patties and cook until the other side is browned and crisp, 5 to 7 minutes more.

Serve the cod cakes garnished with the lemon wedges and parsley sprigs.

Note: If you have leftover mashed potatoes, you will need about 2 cups.

Brandade-Style Cakes

6 servings

*B*randade is a classic Provençal dish of salt cod, potatoes, garlic, and olive oil. Salt cod is a bit of work and needs advance soaking to prepare and is not always readily available, so these cakes can also be made with fresh cod along with the other traditional ingredients. Accompany with a salad of bitter greens dressed with a good red wine vinaigrette. Serve the cakes with thickly sliced fresh tomatoes or a simple marinara sauce.

1 pound salt cod, preferably boneless (see Note)
1 cup milk
1 bay leaf, broken in half
¾ pound all-purpose potatoes, peeled and cut into chunks
6 cloves garlic, peeled
¼ cup heavy cream
1 tablespoon chopped fresh thyme or 1 teaspoon dried

1 teaspoon freshly ground pepper
Pinch of ground cloves
Pinch of grated nutmeg
5 tablespoons extra-virgin olive oil
1 onion, chopped
½ cup chopped flat-leaf parsley
1 tablespoon lemon juice
1½ cups French bread crumbs
1 egg

Place the salt cod in a pan and cover with cold water. Refrigerate, changing the water three or four times, for at least 12 hours or up to 24 hours. Drain the fish and put the pieces in a heavy skillet or saucepan. Add the milk and bay leaf, then add enough water to barely cover the fish. Cover the pan, bring to a boil, then reduce the heat to medium-low and simmer the fish until it is opaque, about 4 minutes. Drain the fish, discarding the cooking liquid and the bay leaf. Remove and discard any bones and skin from the fish, then place it in a large mixing bowl and use your hands to finely flake the fish.

Cook the potatoes and garlic cloves in boiling salted water to cover until very tender, about 20 minutes. Drain well and mash with the heavy cream, thyme, pepper, cloves, and nutmeg. Add to the fish in the mixing bowl.

In a large skillet, heat 1 tablespoon of the oil and cook the onion over medium heat, stirring occasionally, until tender, about 5 minutes.

Add the onion to the mixing bowl, but do not wash the skillet. Add the parsley, lemon juice, ¾ cup of the bread crumbs, and egg to the mixing bowl. Use your hands to gently but thoroughly combine the ingredients.

Divide the mixture into 6 portions, forming each into a patty between 3 and 4 inches in diameter. Place the remaining ¾ cup bread crumbs on a plate and dredge the patties to coat both sides. Refrigerate on a baking sheet for 15 minutes. (Fish cakes can be assembled up to 4 hours ahead to this point and refrigerated.)

Heat the remaining 4 tablespoons oil in the skillet and cook the patties over medium heat until the bottom is browned and crisp, 5 to 7 minutes. Use a spatula to carefully turn the patties and cook until the other side is browned and crisp, 5 to 7 minutes more.

Note: If you use fresh cod fillets, omit the soaking and simply begin by poaching the fish for about 10 minutes until it is cooked through.

Vegetarian Loaves

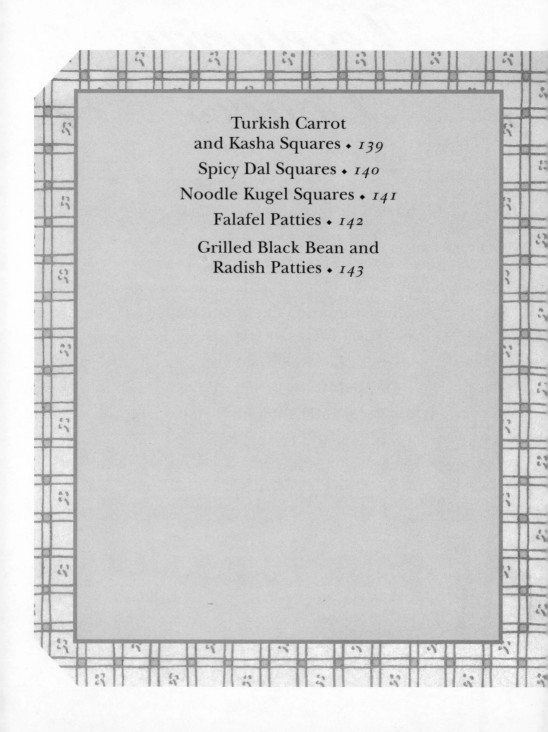

Vegetarian Loaves

Move over meat. Beans, grains, and starchy vegetables are the big news in loaves. Substantial, healthful, wholesome, and hospitable to seasoning, they make sturdy loaves that have nearly unlimited potential for flavorings with cheese, herbs, and other vegetables. And because rice, beans, potatoes, and pasta always seem to be the main leftovers in my refrigerator, these loaves often start with fully prepared ingredients that shorten recipe preparation time considerably.

High in fiber and flavor, full of nutrients, and virtually fat free, beans are showing up on the American table in more ways than baked. In fact, many more members of the legume family, until recently found only in ethnic markets and health food stores, are now far more popular and available in mainstream supermarkets. Now the convenience of canned cooked beans ranges from white cannellini to black beans, with pink, yellow, and red in between. The variety of dried beans is even greater, and they are economical and easy to cook, too.

Grains have also increased their presence on our tables. In fact, the shelf space devoted to grains seems to have at least tripled in recent years. Arborio rice, once nearly impossible to find outside of an Italian market, is commonplace as are all sorts of other rices from basmati to brown and grains from stone-ground cornmeal to kasha. All are full of flavor, and are inexpensive and versatile, too.

Starchy vegetables such as potatoes and corn, as well as many pasta shapes, can also bake into firm, flavorful loaves, especially when bound together and enriched with eggs and/or dairy products.

Some of these loaves are variations on familiar themes, from baked polenta to noodle kugel, while others are simplified interpretations of international favorites, from falafel to molded kasha. All are unusually delicious.

Refried Bean and Pepper Loaf

6 servings

*R*egular, low-fat, or vegetarian refried beans all work well here, as will 4 cups of homemade refried beans, if you happen to have them on hand. You can vary the heat with the amount of jalapeños that you use.

2 tablespoons olive oil
1 onion, chopped
1 green bell pepper, chopped
1 red bell pepper, chopped
3 cloves garlic, minced
1 or 2 jalapeño chiles, seeded
   and minced
1 tablespoon chili powder

1 teaspoon ground cumin
2 cans (1 pound each) refried
   beans
1 cup cooked white rice
⅓ cup chopped cilantro
3 eggs, beaten
1 cup (4 ounces) grated Monterey
   Jack cheese

Preheat the oven to 350 degrees. In a large skillet, heat the oil and cook the onion and bell peppers over medium heat until the vegetables are just softened, about 4 minutes. Add the garlic, jalapeños, chili powder, and cumin. Stir in the beans, rice, cilantro, and eggs.

Spoon the mixture into a 9 by 5-inch loaf pan. Bake for 30 minutes, then sprinkle the cheese over the top. Continue to bake until the loaf is firm and the cheese is bubbly, 25 to 30 minutes longer.

Let the loaf stand in the pan for at least 10 minutes before slicing to serve.

Leftovers: Cold slices are good topped with sliced tomatoes, shredded lettuce, additional grated Jack cheese, and bottled salsa.

Tuscan Polenta Loaf

6 servings

*P*olenta can be soft like mashed potatoes or crusty and firm like a cornmeal focaccia. Here it becomes a cheesy supper loaf, and is particularly delicious sauced with Meatloaf Marinara Sauce or a good-quality bottled pasta sauce flavored with basil.

3 cups yellow cornmeal
3 cups cold water
6 cups reduced-sodium chicken broth
2 cloves garlic, thinly sliced
3 tablespoons unsalted butter
1 cup grated Parmesan cheese

3 tablespoons chopped fresh sage or 1 tablespoon dried
2 eggs
2 ounces thinly sliced prosciutto, optional
Meatloaf Marinara Sauce (page 153) or a good-quality bottled sauce

Butter a shallow 2-quart baking pan. In a mixing bowl, whisk together the cornmeal and cold water. In a heavy 3-quart saucepan, bring the broth and garlic to a boil. Slowly whisk in the cornmeal mixture. Reduce the heat to low and cook, stirring often, until the mixture is very thick and leaves the side of the pan, 15 to 20 minutes. Stir in the butter, cheese, and sage until smooth. In a small bowl, whisk the eggs, then whisk in about 1 cup of the cornmeal mixture to warm the eggs. Whisk the egg mixture into the polenta in the saucepan. Spoon the mixture into the prepared baking pan. (The loaf can be prepared up to 6 hours ahead to this point and refrigerated.)

Preheat the oven to 350 degrees. If using the prosciutto, arrange it over the top of the loaf. Bake until the loaf is firm, pulls away from the sides of the pan, and the prosciutto is frizzled, about 45 minutes. Heat the marinara sauce.

Let the loaf stand in the pan for at least 10 minutes before cutting into squares to serve with the marinara sauce spooned over.

Everybody Loves Meatloaf

Greek Spinach Squares

6 servings

A salad of chopped tomatoes and black olives is a good accompaniment to these squares that are reminiscent of spanakopita without the bother of the phyllo pastry. You can, of course, add the pastry back into the meal if you serve baklava for dessert.

6 eggs
8 ounces (1 cup) cottage cheese
2 tablespoons uncooked farina
(cream of wheat)
6 ounces (1½ cups) crumbled
feta cheese

1 cup cooked white rice
¾ cup chopped scallions
¼ cup chopped flat-leaf parsley
¼ cup chopped fresh dill
½ teaspoon freshly ground
pepper

Preheat the oven to 350 degrees. Coat a shallow 2-quart baking pan with olive oil or nonstick olive oil spray. In a large mixing bowl, whisk the eggs to blend, then whisk in the cottage cheese and farina. Stir in the remaining ingredients.

Spoon the mixture into the prepared pan, smoothing the top. Bake until the loaf is set and the top is crusty, 50 to 55 minutes. Let stand for at least 10 minutes before cutting into squares to serve.

Leftovers: Serve room temperature squares on romaine leaves garnished with tomato wedges and an assortment of Mediterranean olives.

Leek and Golden Potato Squares

6 servings

Yukon Gold potatoes are particularly attractive for their buttery yellow color, but other thin-skinned potatoes can be used in this recipe if you can't find them. In fact, any leftover cooked and sliced potatoes will work well.

1 pound Yukon Gold potatoes, cut
    into 2-inch chunks
3 tablespoons unsalted butter
4 cups thinly sliced leeks,
    including light green parts
    (5 to 6 medium leeks)
12 eggs

2 tablespoons chopped fresh
    tarragon or 2 teaspoons dried
¾ teaspoon salt
¾ teaspoon freshly ground pepper
¼ teaspoon grated nutmeg
1 cup (4 ounces) shredded Gruyère
    or Swiss cheese

Cook the potatoes in boiling salted water to cover until just tender, about 2 minutes. Drain the potatoes and cool until they can be handled. Peel and thinly slice the potatoes and set aside.

Preheat the oven to 375 degrees. Use 1 tablespoon of the butter to generously grease a shallow 2-quart baking pan. In a large skillet, heat the remaining 2 tablespoons butter and cook the leeks over medium heat, stirring often until softened, about 5 minutes.

In a mixing bowl, whisk together the eggs, tarragon, salt, pepper, and nutmeg.

Spread the potatoes over the bottom of the baking pan, then spoon the leeks over the potatoes. Pour the egg mixture over the leeks, then sprinkle with the cheese.

Bake until the eggs are set and puffed, about 30 minutes. Serve immediately, cut into squares.

Leftovers: The squares will deflate upon cooling, but then they can be cut into 1-inch squares to make a tasty little snack or hors d'oeuvre.

Garlic, Grits, and Greens Squares

6 servings

For truly vegetarian squares, you could leave out the ham, but then you might add about ⅓ cup more grated Parmesan cheese for extra flavor.

3 tablespoons unseasoned dry bread crumbs
1 pound collard greens, trimmed and chopped, or 1 package (10 ounces) chopped frozen collard greens
3 tablespoons unsalted butter
4 ounces smoked ham, cut into ¼-inch dice

4 cloves garlic, minced
3 cups milk
½ teaspoon salt
½ teaspoon freshly ground pepper
¼ teaspoon cayenne
1 cup uncooked quick grits
½ cup grated Parmesan cheese
4 eggs

Preheat the oven to 350 degrees. Generously butter a shallow 2-quart baking pan and sprinkle the bottom and sides with the bread crumbs. Boil or steam the fresh collards until tender, about 5 minutes. Or thaw and squeeze excess moisture from the frozen collards. Set aside.

In a medium skillet, heat 1 tablespoon of the butter and cook the ham over medium-high heat, stirring often until browned, 3 to 5 minutes. Add the garlic and collards and cook, stirring often, 2 minutes more. Set aside.

In a heavy 3-quart saucepan, bring the milk, salt, pepper, and cayenne to a boil. Stir in the grits, reduce the heat to medium-low, and cook, stirring almost constantly until the grits are very thick, 3 to 4 minutes. Stir in the remaining 2 tablespoons butter, cheese, and cooked ham and vegetables. In a small bowl, whisk the eggs, then whisk in about 1 cup of the grits to warm the eggs. Blend the egg mixture back into the grits in the saucepan.

Spoon the grits into the prepared baking pan. Set the pan in a larger pan half-filled with hot water. Bake until firm, puffed, and golden, 45 to 55 minutes. Remove the baking pan from the water bath and let stand for at least 10 minutes before cutting into squares to serve.

Leftovers: The squares become quite firm as they cool and are good served with chopped fresh tomatoes dressed with vinegar and oil.

Crusty Roasted Garlic Risotto Squares

6 servings

*T*like to spread this rather thinly in a 3-quart baking pan so that there will be more of the delicious crusty top. The recipe can be endlessly varied with the addition of cooked vegetables from sliced asparagus to diced zucchini. Almost any leftover risotto can be used here—just beat in 1 egg for every 2 or 3 cups of risotto.

10 garlic cloves, peeled
3 tablespoons extra-virgin olive oil
4 cups canned vegetable broth
2 cups dry white wine
2 cups raw arborio rice

3 cups seeded and diced fresh plum tomatoes, or 2 cans (14½ ounces each) diced tomatoes with liquid
1 cup slivered fresh basil
1 cup grated Parmesan cheese
3 eggs

Preheat the oven to 350 degrees. Butter a shallow 3-quart baking pan.

Place the garlic cloves on a piece of double-thickness aluminum foil and drizzle with 1 tablespoon olive oil. Fold up the foil to enclose the garlic completely. Bake until the garlic is very soft, 25 to 30 minutes. Remove from the oven but do not turn the oven off. Mash the garlic with the back of a spoon.

While the garlic is roasting, bring the vegetable broth, wine, and ⅔ cup water to a simmer in a saucepan. Keep the mixture just below a simmer over low heat. In another heavy 3- or 4-quart saucepan, heat the remaining 2 tablespoons olive oil. Add rice and cook, stirring, for 1 minute over medium heat to coat the grains. Add about 2 cups of the simmering liquid to the rice and cook, stirring often, until most of the liquid is absorbed, about 20 minutes. Continue to add liquid by cupfuls, stirring occasionally until each cup is nearly absorbed before adding another. After about 25 minutes, all of the liquid should be added and the rice should be very thick and creamy. Stir in the tomatoes with their liquid, basil, cheese, and roasted garlic. In a small bowl, whisk the eggs, then whisk in about 1 cup of the risotto to warm the eggs. Return the egg mixture to the saucepan and mix well.

Everybody Loves Meatloaf

Spread the risotto mixture evenly over the bottom of the prepared pan. Bake until the risotto is crusty and golden brown, 45 to 55 minutes. Let stand for at least 10 minutes before cutting into squares to serve.

Leftovers: Chill the squares, then cut into smaller (1-inch) squares to serve as a snack or hors d'oeuvres with Lemon-Caper Sour Cream (page 156) as a dip.

Toasted Corn Pudding Squares

6 servings

*T*hese squares are a cross between a custard pudding and a moist corn bread, and are substantial enough to satisfy as a supper main course that needs little more than a tossed salad.

3 tablespoons butter
1 onion, chopped
1 small red bell pepper, chopped
1 cup fresh, frozen, or canned corn
    kernels
1 cup thinly sliced scallions
1 can (4 ounces) chopped mild
    green chiles, drained
1 cup all-purpose flour
1 cup yellow cornmeal

1 tablespoon sugar
2 teaspoons baking powder
¾ teaspoon salt
½ teaspoon freshly ground pepper
¼ teaspoon cayenne
3 eggs
1 cup low-fat yogurt
½ cup milk
1 cup shredded Monterey
    Jack cheese

Preheat the oven to 350 degrees. Butter a shallow 2-quart baking pan. In a large skillet, heat the butter and cook the onion, red pepper, and corn over medium-high heat, stirring occasionally, until the vegetables are softened and tinged with brown, 6 to 8 minutes. Add the scallions and chiles and cook 1 minute.

In a large mixing bowl, whisk together the flour, cornmeal, sugar, baking powder, salt, pepper, and cayenne. In another mixing bowl, whisk the eggs to blend, then whisk in the yogurt, milk, and cheese. Pour the liquids over the dry ingredients and stir to blend. Add the cooked vegetables and stir just until blended.

Spoon the mixture into the prepared baking pan, smoothing the top. Set the baking pan in a larger pan half-filled with hot water. Bake until firm and golden brown, 45 to 50 minutes. Remove the baking pan from the water bath and let cool for at least 10 minutes before cutting into squares to serve.

Deviled Broccoli Squares

6 servings

*T*n the spring, substitute cooked asparagus for the broccoli, and in the summer, bell peppers are a good choice. If you use leftover vegetables, about 3 cups of diced cooked vegetables is the right amount.

¾ pound broccoli (1 medium bunch)
3 tablespoons butter
1 large onion, chopped
8 ounces French bread, torn into pieces
8 eggs
2 tablespoons Dijon mustard

¾ cup milk
½ teaspoon salt
½ teaspoon freshly ground pepper
¼ teaspoon dried hot pepper flakes
1 cup shredded Cheddar cheese
3 tablespoons grated Parmesan cheese

Preheat the oven to 350 degrees. Generously butter a shallow 2-quart baking pan. Trim the broccoli, slicing the stems and separating the florets into bite-sized pieces. Cook the broccoli in boiling salted water to cover until just tender, 4 to 5 minutes. Drain well. In a large skillet, heat the butter and cook the onion over medium heat, stirring occasionally, until softened, about 5 minutes. Stir in the broccoli.

Arrange the bread in the baking pan, spoon the broccoli mixture over the bread, and stir to mix in. In a mixing bowl, whisk the eggs, then whisk in the mustard, milk, salt, pepper, pepper flakes, and Cheddar cheese. Pour over the bread mixture, pressing the bread into the liquid. Sprinkle with the Parmesan cheese.

Bake until the loaf is set and the top is puffed and golden brown, 45 to 55 minutes. Serve immediately.

White Bean and Spaghetti Squares

6 to 8 servings

*T*his is an ideal use for leftover spaghetti or any other strand pasta. It becomes the crust for the savory squares that, with a change from Italian-seasoned to chile-style stewed tomatoes and from mozzarella to Monterey Jack cheese, can turn this Italian-style supper into a Mexican fiesta. Kids are guaranteed to love this one.

Crust
3½ to 4 cups cooked spaghetti
   (about ½ pound uncooked)
½ cup milk
1 egg
¼ cup grated Romano cheese
Filling
2 tablespoons olive oil
1 large onion, chopped
1 small red bell pepper, chopped
1 small yellow bell pepper,
   chopped

2 cloves garlic, minced
2 tablespoons chopped fresh
   oregano or 2 teaspoons dried
¼ cup chopped fresh basil
½ cup milk
3 eggs
1 can (1 pound) white beans,
   rinsed and drained
1 can (14½ ounces) Italian-style
   stewed tomatoes with juice
2 cups (8 ounces) grated mozzarella
   cheese

Coat a shallow 3-quart baking pan with nonstick olive oil spray. If the pasta is cold, reheat it in a microwave oven, then place it in the prepared pan. Add the milk, egg, and Romano cheese, mixing well. Spread the mixture to cover the bottom and about 1 inch up the sides of the prepared pan. Set aside.

Preheat the oven to 375 degrees. In a large skillet, heat the oil and cook the onion and red and yellow bell peppers over medium heat, stirring occasionally, until the vegetables are just softened, about 4 minutes. Add the garlic, oregano, and basil, and cook 1 minute more. In a small bowl, whisk the milk with the eggs to blend. Stir the egg mixture and beans into the cooked vegetables in the skillet. Spoon the filling into the prepared spaghetti "crust." Spread the tomatoes over the top, then sprinkle with the cheese.

Cover with aluminum foil and bake for 15 minutes. Uncover and bake until the filling is set and the cheese is melted and bubbly, 20 to 25 minutes more. (The recipe can be assembled up to 8 hours ahead and refrigerated. Increase covered baking time by 10 minutes, then uncover and continue to bake as directed.)

Let stand for 10 minutes before cutting into squares to serve.

Leftovers: If you like cold spaghetti for breakfast, this is your loaf!

Green Rice and Fennel Squares

6 servings

*F*ennel is a most aromatic vegetable, tasting of mild licorice. It is particularly well suited to tomatoes, so a saucing of Meatloaf Marinara Sauce (page 153), Tomato-Citrus Chutney (page 156), or chunked fresh tomatoes will provide a colorful, tasty accompaniment.

2 tablespoons olive oil
2 cups diced fresh fennel (about ½ pound)
¾ cup chopped scallions
½ cup chopped flat-leaf parsley
¾ teaspoon salt
½ teaspoon freshly ground pepper

½ teaspoon grated lemon peel
6 eggs
2½ cups cooked white rice
4 ounces (1 cup) shredded mozzarella cheese
1½ cups Meatloaf Marinara Sauce, Tomato-Citrus Chutney, or chunked fresh tomatoes

Preheat the oven to 350 degrees. Coat a shallow 2-quart baking pan with olive oil or olive oil nonstick spray. In a large skillet, heat the oil and cook the fennel over medium heat, stirring occasionally, until just softened, about 4 minutes. Add the scallions and parsley and cook 1 minute. Stir in the salt, pepper, and lemon peel.

In a large mixing bowl, whisk the eggs to blend. Then, stir in the cooked vegetables, rice, and cheese. Pat the mixture into the prepared pan. Bake until the top is crusty and rich golden brown, 50 to 60 minutes.

Let stand in the baking pan for at least 10 minutes before cutting into squares to serve with the desired sauce.

Leftovers: This is good served cold with the same saucing as above.

Turkish Carrot and Kasha Squares

6 servings

*K*asha, toasted buckwheat groats, has a pleasing nutty flavor and meaty texture. It's especially well suited to making a good loaf.

1½ cups kasha
3 cups canned chicken broth, regular or reduced-sodium
2 tablespoons butter
1 large onion, chopped
6 carrots, cut into ¼-inch dice
6 cloves garlic, minced
1 teaspoon ground allspice
1 teaspoon ground cumin

1 teaspoon ground coriander
½ teaspoon cayenne
½ teaspoon salt (see Note)
½ cup chopped dates or dried cherries
⅓ cup chopped flat-leaf parsley
⅓ cup chopped fresh mint
4 eggs

In a large saucepan, toss the kasha over medium-high heat for 1 minute until slightly fragrant. Stir in the broth and bring to a boil. Reduce the heat to medium-low and simmer until the liquid is absorbed, about 15 minutes. (The kasha can be cooked a day ahead and refrigerated.)

Preheat the oven to 350 degrees. Butter a shallow 2-quart baking pan or coat with nonstick vegetable spray. In a large skillet, heat the butter and cook the onion and carrots over medium heat, stirring occasionally, until the onion is soft and the carrot is just tender, 6 to 8 minutes. Stir in the garlic, allspice, cumin, coriander, cayenne, and salt.

In a large mixing bowl, use your hands to combine the kasha, cooked vegetables, dates, parsley, mint, and eggs. Pat the mixture into the prepared pan. Bake until the loaf is firm and the top is crusty brown, about 50 minutes.

Let the loaf stand in the pan for at least 10 minutes before cutting into squares to serve.

Leftovers: Serve cold slices on a bed of romaine lettuce dolloped with yogurt and sprinkled with chopped red onion.

Note: If using reduced-sodium broth, increase the salt to 1 teaspoon.

Spicy Dal Squares

6 servings

*L*entils have a wonderful hearty texture and are a terrific meat substitute. They are an ideal base upon which a very spicy dish can be built, as demonstrated in this simplified version of an Indian dish.

1½ cups dry lentils
3 cups canned vegetable broth or
  salted water
2 tablespoons olive oil
1 onion, chopped
1 small red bell pepper
10 ounces torn raw spinach,
  steamed until tender and
  drained, or 1 package (9 ounces)
  frozen chopped spinach, thawed
  and well squeezed
3 cloves garlic, minced

2 tablespoons finely chopped
  fresh ginger
½ teaspoon salt
½ teaspoon turmeric
½ teaspoon cayenne
½ teaspoon ground cinnamon
½ teaspoon ground cardamom
¼ teaspoon ground cloves
¼ cup chopped flat-leaf
  parsley
¼ cup chopped cilantro
4 eggs

Place the lentils and the broth or water in a 2- or 3-quart saucepan. Bring to a boil, cover the pan, reduce the heat to medium-low, and simmer until the lentils are tender and the liquid is absorbed, 30 to 40 minutes. (If the lentils seem too dry, add a little more water toward the end of the cooking time.)

Preheat the oven to 350 degrees. Butter a shallow 2-quart baking pan or coat with olive oil nonstick cooking spray. Heat the oil and cook the onion and bell pepper over medium heat, stirring occasionally, until the vegetables are just softened, about 4 minutes. Add the spinach, garlic, and ginger. Cook, stirring, 1 minute. Stir in the salt, turmeric, cayenne, cinnamon, cardamom, and cloves.

In a large mixing bowl, use your hands to combine the lentils, cooked vegetable mixture, parsley, cilantro, and eggs. Pat the mixture into the prepared pan, smoothing the top. Bake until the loaf is firm and the top is crusty brown, about 1 hour.

Let stand in the baking pan for 10 minutes before cutting into squares to serve.

Noodle Kugel Squares

6 servings

*N*oodle kugel is too good to be relegated to side dish status. As a main dish, this kugel has ample protein, plenty of carbohydrates, and lots of flavor. A square of kugel and a big green salad is a wonderfully simple and warming supper on a cool evening.

½ cup chopped mixed dried fruit
1 tablespoon all-purpose flour
½ teaspoon ground cinnamon
½ teaspoon grated nutmeg
½ teaspoon salt
½ teaspoon freshly ground
* pepper*
3 eggs

1½ cups cottage cheese
1½ cups half and half or
* whole milk*
½ cup sour cream, regular or
* reduced-fat*
3 cups cooked egg noodles
* (6 ounces uncooked)*
¼ cup sliced almonds

Preheat the oven to 350 degrees. Butter a shallow 2-quart baking pan. In a small bowl, toss together the dried fruit, flour, cinnamon, nutmeg, salt, and pepper. In a large mixing bowl, whisk the eggs, then blend in the cottage cheese, half and half, and sour cream. Stir in the fruit mixture and the noodles.

Spoon the mixture into the prepared baking pan, smoothing the top. Sprinkle with the almonds.

Bake until the kugel is set and the top is light golden, 45 to 55 minutes. Let stand in the baking pan for at least 10 minutes before cutting into squares to serve.

Leftovers: You can turn leftover chilled squares into dessert by drizzling them with maple syrup or honey.

Falafel Patties

6 servings

*F*ried mashed chickpea patties are "street food" in much of the Middle East. They are stuffed into pita breads and served with spicy tomato-based sauces, such as Tomato-Citrus Chutney (page 156), or with Cucumber-Yogurt Sauce (page 155).

1 onion, cut into chunks
1 cup parsley sprigs
4 cloves garlic, peeled
2 cans (16 ounces each) chickpeas, rinsed and drained
2 teaspoons grated orange peel
2 teaspoons ground cumin
1½ teaspoons ground coriander
½ teaspoon cayenne

½ teaspoon ground turmeric
¼ teaspoon ground cinnamon
½ teaspoon ground allspice
½ teaspoon salt
4 tablespoons olive oil
6 pita breads
2 cups Tomato-Citrus Chutney, optional
1½ cups Cucumber-Yogurt Sauce, optional

Place the onion and parsley in a food processor. With the motor running, drop the garlic cloves through the feed tube and process just until the onion is chopped. Add the chickpeas, orange peel, cumin, coriander, cayenne, turmeric, cinnamon, allspice, and salt. Pulse to process just until the chickpeas are coarsely ground and the spices are blended in.

Divide the mixture into 12 portions, forming each into a patty 3 or 4 inches in diameter and about ½ inch thick. In a large skillet, heat half of the oil over medium heat. Fry half of the patties until browned on the bottom, about 5 minutes. Turn carefully with a spatula and fry until the other side is browned, about 5 minutes more. Use the remaining oil to fry the remaining patties. (If desired, keep the first batch warm in a single layer in a 300-degree oven while you are frying the second batch.)

Stuff 2 falafel patties into each pita bread and garnish with the Tomato-Citrus Chutney and/or Cucumber-Yogurt Sauce.

Grilled Black Bean and Radish Patties

6 servings

*T*his is a great way to use leftover cooked black beans, though canned beans work just as well, too. The radishes add a peppery zip and attractive red fleck to these tasty vegetarian patties. They can also be cooked indoors in a skillet in 1 to 2 tablespoons of vegetable oil. The patties are good plain or stuffed into pita pockets.

1 cup plus 2 tablespoons plain yogurt
6 tablespoons bottled mango chutney
2 tablespoons chopped cilantro
1 tablespoon vegetable oil
¾ cup chopped red onion
3½ cups cooked black beans or 2 cans (16 ounces each) black beans, rinsed and drained

½ cup plain dry bread crumbs
¼ cup coarsely grated radishes
2 teaspoons curry powder
1 teaspoon ground cumin
½ teaspoon ground cardamom
½ teaspoon ground coriander
½ teaspoon salt
¼ teaspoon ground ginger
⅛ teaspoon cayenne
Radish sprouts for garnish

In a small bowl, stir together 1 cup of the yogurt, 4 tablespoons of the chutney, and the cilantro. Refrigerate for at least 30 minutes or up to 24 hours before using. In a small skillet, heat the oil and cook the onion over medium heat, stirring often until soft, about 5 minutes.

Prepare a medium-hot barbecue fire or preheat a gas grill. Oil the grill rack or coat with nonstick vegetable spray.

In a food processor, pulse to coarsely mash together the beans, bread crumbs, grated radishes, curry powder, cumin, cardamom, coriander, salt, ginger, cayenne, the remaining 2 tablespoons each of yogurt and chutney, and the cooked onion.

Divide the mixture into 6 parts, forming each into a patty 3 to 4 inches in diameter and about ½ inch thick. Grill until crusty and brown on the bottom, about 5 minutes. Using a spatula, carefully turn the patties and grill until browned, about 5 minutes more.

Serve the patties dolloped with the seasoned yogurt and sprinkled with the radish sprouts.

Sauces, Condiments, and a Great

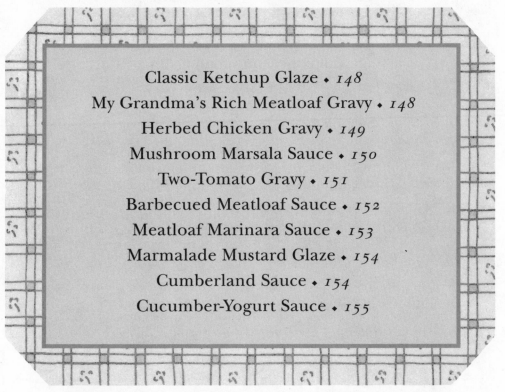

Mashed Potato

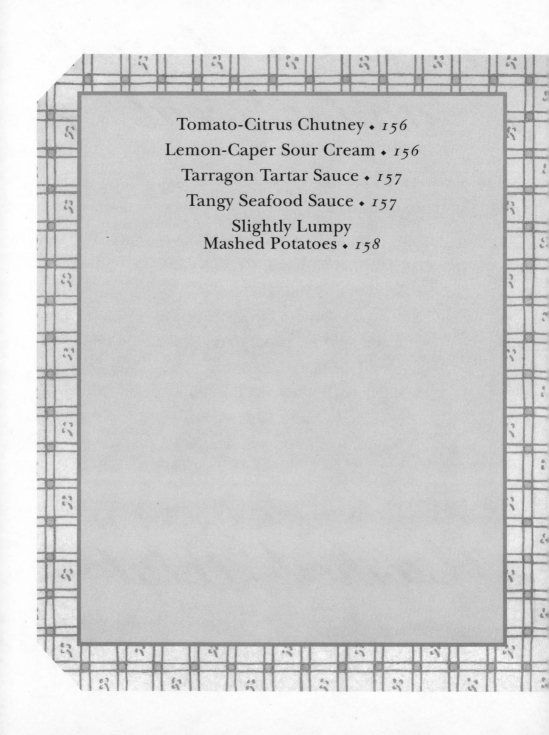

Sauces, Condiments, and a Great Mashed Potato

One of the best things about a meat, poultry, seafood, or vegetarian loaf is that it is practically a one-dish meal containing protein, starch, and often vegetables, too. But as any good cook knows, it is possible to gild the culinary lily with a glaze, a sauce, or a condiment. These complement and enhance a well-prepared dish, but can never cover up shortcomings or shortcuts.

The sauces presented here are versatile and easy to make. Some of the loaf recipes specifically recommend a certain sauce, but use your tasteful imagination to pair a loaf and a sauce in new ways I may not have considered.

My favorite recipe for mashed potatoes is also in this section. Though not a sauce or a condiment, I cannot imagine a meatloaf cookbook without a mashed potato recipe.

Classic Ketchup Glaze

Makes about ½ cup

The onion will cook in the oven so there is no need to sauté it before adding to the sauce. This may seem like a nonrecipe because it is so easy, but the few added ingredients vastly improve plain ketchup as a glaze.

⅓ cup tomato ketchup
3 tablespoons finely chopped onion
   or shallots

2 teaspoons lemon juice or red
   wine vinegar
¼ teaspoon freshly ground pepper

In a small bowl, stir together all the ingredients. Use immediately or refrigerate up to 2 days before using.

My Grandma's Rich Meatloaf Gravy

Makes about 1¾ cups

My grandma made a really good, though very simple, meatloaf. She also made a good gravy for her meatloaf. Note that Grandma also believed in a "spot" of sherry now and then, too.

1 tablespoon unsalted butter
2 tablespoons all-purpose flour
1¾ cups beef broth, homemade or
   reduced-sodium canned

1 tablespoon dry sherry
2 teaspoons tomato paste
¼ teaspoon freshly ground pepper
Salt to taste

In a heavy saucepan, heat the butter over medium heat and stir in the flour to make a smooth paste. Continue to cook and stir for 1 to 2 minutes until the paste begins to brown and has a nutty aroma. Slowly whisk in the broth, sherry, tomato paste, and pepper. Slowly bring to a boil, whisking or stirring constantly. Reduce the heat to medium-low and simmer for 3 to 5 minutes. Season to taste with salt.

Herbed Chicken Gravy

Makes about 1¾ cups

*T*buy a lot of cut-up chickens, but rarely use the giblets that come in the package. But my Yankee thriftiness prevents me from tossing them away, so I always have plenty of giblets in the freezer and use them to enhance gravy made from canned chicken broth. The pinch of allspice makes a big difference.

Giblets from 1 chicken
1¾ cups chicken broth,
homemade or reduced-sodium
canned
1 tablespoon unsalted butter
2 tablespoons all-purpose flour

1 tablespoon chopped fresh herbs,
such as thyme, sage, rosemary, or
marjoram, or 1 teaspoon dried
¼ teaspoon freshly ground pepper
Small pinch of ground allspice
Salt to taste

In a small saucepan, simmer the giblets in the broth until they are no longer pink, about 20 minutes. Remove the giblets with a slotted spoon, chop them, and return to the broth. Set aside.

In a heavy saucepan, heat the butter over medium heat and stir in the flour to make a smooth paste. Continue to cook and stir until the flour begins to turn golden and has a nutty fragrance, 1 to 2 minutes more. Whisk in the broth and giblets, slowly bringing to a boil, whisking constantly. Reduce the heat to medium-low and add the herbs, pepper, and allspice. Simmer, stirring often, for 3 minutes. Season to taste with salt.

Mushroom Marsala Sauce

Makes about 2 cups

*W*ild mushrooms are especially wonderful here, particularly shiitake mushrooms, but a mix of wild and button mushrooms also provides excellent flavor at less cost. This is terrific with almost any meat or poultry loaf, and can be customized with either beef or chicken broth and the herb selection.

2 tablespoons unsalted butter

6 ounces (about 2 cups) sliced mushrooms, wild or button or a combination

2 tablespoons finely chopped shallots

1 tablespoon all-purpose flour

1½ cups beef or chicken broth, homemade or reduced-sodium canned

2 tablespoons Marsala wine

1 tablespoon chopped fresh herbs, such as tarragon, sage, or thyme, or 1 teaspoon dried

Salt and freshly ground pepper to taste

In a large skillet or wide-bottomed saucepan, heat the butter and cook the mushrooms and shallots over medium-low heat, stirring often, until the mushrooms are soft and have given up their liquid, about 5 minutes. Raise the heat to medium and cook, stirring often, until about half of the liquid is evaporated, about 2 minutes. Stir in the flour and cook, stirring, for 1 minute. Whisk in the broth, Marsala, and herbs. Bring to a boil, stirring. Reduce the heat to medium-low and simmer, stirring often, for 3 minutes. Season to taste with salt and pepper.

Everybody Loves Meatloaf

Two-Tomato Gravy

Makes about 2 cups

*T*he addition of a bit of cream smoothes out this spicy sauce, which is good with plain meat or poultry loaves, and Mediterranean-style seafood or vegetable loaves.

2 tablespoons chopped sun-dried tomatoes in oil plus 2 teaspoons of the packing oil
2 teaspoons extra-virgin olive oil
1 clove garlic, minced
1 can (14½ ounces) diced tomatoes with juices

¼ cup dry red wine
⅛ teaspoon dried hot pepper flakes
1 tablespoon chopped fresh oregano or marjoram or 1 teaspoon dried
2 tablespoons heavy cream
Salt to taste

In a saucepan, heat the sun-dried tomato oil and olive oil over medium heat and cook the garlic, stirring, for 1 minute. Add the sun-dried tomatoes, canned tomatoes with juices, wine, pepper flakes, and dried herb. Simmer, stirring often, until slightly reduced, about 8 minutes. Stir in the cream and fresh herb, if using. Simmer 2 minutes. Season to taste with salt.

Barbecued Meatloaf Sauce

Makes about 2 cups

*T*here are several good bottled barbecue sauces on the market today, and if you doctor them up a bit many will rival homemade sauces. For this recipe, I particularly like to begin with a sauce that has a light hickory flavor. Brush onto Barbecued Meatloaves (page 37) or use to glaze the top of many home-style meat or poultry loaves baked in the oven. It is also an easy way to make a homemade all-purpose barbecue sauce, which you can then further personalize with the addition of herbs or spices if you wish.

1 cup bottled barbecue sauce,
  regular or hickory-flavored
½ cup bottled chili sauce
½ cup beer or ginger ale

1 tablespoon Worcestershire
  sauce
1 small onion, finely chopped
2 cloves garlic, minced

In a medium saucepan, simmer all the ingredients together over medium-low heat until slightly thickened, about 10 minutes.

Use immediately or refrigerate up to a week.

Meatloaf Marinara Sauce

Makes about 2 cups

*W*ith the advent of good-quality canned diced tomatoes, homemade marinara sauce can be made year-round in about 10 minutes. Use it with all sorts of Italian-style meat and poultry loaves. Or, change the herb to cilantro, add a chopped jalapeño, and use it with Mexican-style loaves.

1 tablespoon extra-virgin olive oil
1 small onion, chopped
1 clove garlic, minced
1 can (14½ ounces) diced tomatoes with juices
⅓ cup dry white wine

½ teaspoon freshly ground pepper
2 tablespoons chopped fresh basil
2 tablespoons chopped flat-leaf parsley
Salt to taste

In a saucepan, heat the oil over medium heat and cook the onion and garlic, stirring often, for 3 minutes, until they begin to soften. Add the tomatoes and juices, wine, and pepper. Simmer, stirring often, until slightly reduced, about 8 minutes. Stir in the basil and parsley. Season to taste with salt. Use immediately or refrigerate up to 4 days. (If you would like to make the sauce ahead, do not add the herbs until you reheat it to serve.)

Marmalade Mustard Glaze

Makes about ½ cup

*U*se this simple glaze for many ham or pork loaves. It's also a good savory dipping sauce for raw apple slices.

¼ cup Dijon mustard
3 tablespoons orange marmalade
1 tablespoon orange juice

1 tablespoon lemon juice
2 teaspoons reduced-sodium soy sauce

In a small saucepan over medium-low heat, gently simmer together all the ingredients, stirring often, for 2 minutes. Use immediately or refrigerate up to 4 days.

Cumberland Sauce

Makes about 1 cup

*T*his is a simplified version of a classic British sauce served with game. It is excellent with venison loaves, and with pork loaves with fruit.

½ cup port wine
½ cup currant jelly
2 tablespoons lemon juice
2 teaspoons dry mustard

1 teaspoon ground ginger
Pinch of ground cloves
2 teaspoons grated orange peel

In a medium saucepan, simmer all of the ingredients together until slightly reduced, about 5 minutes. The sauce can be made several days ahead and refrigerated. Reheat to use.

Cucumber-Yogurt Sauce

Makes about 1½ cups

*T*hickened yogurt is a versatile base for all sorts of dips and is the main ingredient in tzatziki, the classic Greek and Turkish cucumber-yogurt sauce. Use this cooling sauce as a condiment for spicy seafood, lamb, or vegetarian loaves.

2 cups plain yogurt
1 small cucumber, seeded and
* coarsely chopped*
½ teaspoon salt
2 tablespoons chopped scallion
* greens*

2 tablespoons chopped fresh mint
1 large clove garlic, minced
1 tablespoon extra-virgin olive oil
2 teaspoons lemon juice
Freshly ground pepper

Spoon the yogurt into a cheesecloth-lined sieve and set over a bowl. Refrigerate for 4 to 6 hours, then discard the drained liquid and place the thickened yogurt in a bowl. Meanwhile, place the cucumber in another sieve or colander and sprinkle with the salt. Let stand for 30 minutes to draw out excess moisture.

In a bowl, gently stir together the thickened yogurt, cucumber, scallion greens, mint, garlic, oil, and lemon juice. Season to taste with pepper.

Refrigerate for at least 15 minutes or up to 8 hours before serving.

Tomato-Citrus Chutney

Makes about 2 cups

*C*hutneys can be raw or cooked, and usually are a spicy combination of fruits and vegetables. This very easy one depends on good fresh tomatoes, so reserve it for summer. Serve with any Indian- or Middle Eastern–style meat, poultry, or vegetable loaf.

2 cups seeded and diced fresh
   plum tomatoes
¼ cup chopped shallots
¼ cup chopped fresh mint
1½ tablespoons extra-virgin
   olive oil
1 tablespoon lemon juice

1 tablespoon orange juice
2 teaspoons grated lemon peel
2 teaspoons grated orange peel
½ teaspoon salt
½ teaspoon cayenne
½ teaspoon ground coriander

In a mixing bowl, combine all the ingredients. Let stand at least 30 minutes at room temperature or refrigerate up to 12 hours before serving.

Lemon-Caper Sour Cream

Makes about ¾ cup

*T*his sauce can be endlessly varied with the addition of 1 tablespoon chopped fresh herbs, such as dill, tarragon, or basil. It is particularly good with seafood loaves.

¾ cup sour cream, regular or
   low-fat
1 tablespoon drained small capers

2 teaspoons grated lemon peel
¼ teaspoon salt
¼ teaspoon freshly ground pepper

In a small bowl, stir together all the ingredients. Refrigerate for at least 30 minutes or up to 2 days before serving.

Tarragon Tartar Sauce

Makes about 1 cup

*O*ther herbs can be used, but tarragon seems to be just right for most seafood cakes and loaves. This sauce is also good with poultry loaves and even as a spread for sandwiches or a salad dressing.

*¾ cup mayonnaise, regular or
low-fat*
*2 tablespoons sweet pickle relish,
such as India relish*

*1½ tablespoons chopped fresh
tarragon or 1 teaspoon dried*
2 teaspoons lemon juice
¼ teaspoon hot pepper sauce

In a small mixing bowl, whisk or stir together all the ingredients. Cover and refrigerate at least 1 hour or up to 3 days before using.

Tangy Seafood Sauce

Makes about 1 cup

*A*n easy homemade version of bottled seafood cocktail sauce, this one has the zing of fresh-grated horseradish. Personalize the flavor with different herbs.

¾ cup bottled tomato ketchup
*3 tablespoons chopped flat-leaf
parsley*
*2 tablespoons grated fresh
horseradish*

*1 tablespoon Worcestershire
sauce*
*1 tablespoon chopped fresh thyme,
cilantro, or oregano*
½ teaspoon hot pepper sauce

In a mixing bowl, stir or whisk together all ingredients. Refrigerate at least 1 hour or up to 3 days before using.

Slightly Lumpy Mashed Potatoes

6 to 8 servings (about 7 cups)

*T*here are endless contemporary versions of mashed potatoes. You could add chopped herbs or cook a few garlic cloves along with the potatoes and then mash them together. Personally, I like all of these variations, but not with meatloaf. Meatloaf calls for plain mashed potatoes. I like my potatoes with a few lumps, but you can beat them until perfectly smooth if you prefer. In addition, I do succumb to the contemporary twist of using part Yukon Gold potatoes when I can find them. Their gold color is so pretty and gives the effect of buttery mashed potatoes without so much butter. Adjust the butter and use yogurt or sour cream depending upon your preferences.

3 pounds all-purpose potatoes (half Yukon Gold, if desired), peeled and cut into chunks
2 to 3 tablespoons unsalted butter

⅔ cup milk
¼ cup sour cream, light sour cream, or plain yogurt
Salt and freshly ground pepper to taste

Cook the potatoes in a pot of salted boiling water to cover until they are very tender, about 20 minutes. Meanwhile, in a small saucepan, heat the butter and milk over low heat until the butter is melted.

Drain the cooked potatoes well and return the potatoes to the cooking pot set over medium-low heat. Stir the potatoes over the heat for 1 minute to further dry them. Remove the pan from the heat and use a handheld electric mixer or a ricer to coarsely mash the potatoes. Add the heated milk mixture and the sour cream and continue to mash until nearly smooth and fluffy. Season to taste with salt and pepper.

Leftovers: Leftover mashed potatoes can be used wherever mashed potatoes are called for in a meatloaf recipe. They can also be made into wonderful potato cakes. Use your hands to shape them into small flat cakes no more than ½ inch thick. Dip the cakes lightly in flour to coat, then fry them in a little butter or oil until browned on both sides.

Index

159

truck-stop turkey loaf, 68
tuna:
  melt loaf, Southwest, 114
  vitello tonnato loaf, 30
turkey, ground, 2–3
  in bistro chicken liver loaf, 85
  in dirty rice loaf, 84
  in sauerkraut and turkey kielbasa
    loaf, 71
turkey kielbasa and sauerkraut loaf, 71
turkey loaf (loaves):
  Cajun grilled, 96
  grilled dilled, 98
  heritage chestnut and, 74
  and jalapeño corn bread squares,
    93
  Lindstrom, 76
  mole, 78
  paprikash squares, 91
  picadillo squares, 92
  sage stuffing and, 69
  scrapple, 77
  shiitake and, with sherry gravy, 72–73
  sun-dried tomato pesto and, 70
  tarragon hash, 75
  truck-stop, 68
  turkey club squares, 90
  wild rice and, 89
Turkish carrot and kasha squares,
  139
turnovers, meatloaf pasties, 38
Tuscan polenta loaf, 128
Tuscan turkey loaves, grilled, 97
two-tomato gravy, 151

veal, ground, 2
  see also meatloaf mix
veal loaf (loaves):
  grilled meatloaves provençal, 36

osso buco loaf with gremolata
  tomato gravy, 25
pork and, rollatini, 47
Sicilian braciole loaf, 28
vitello tonnato loaf, 30
vegetable, summer, and chicken loaf,
  86–87
vegetarian loaves, 123–43
  basic, 3
  crusty roasted garlic risotto squares,
    132–33
  deviled broccoli squares, 135
  falafel patties, 142
  garlic, grits and greens squares, 131
  Greek spinach squares, 129
  green rice and fennel squares, 138
  leek and golden potato squares, 130
  noodle kugel squares, 141
  spicy dal squares, 140
  toasted corn pudding squares, 134
  Turkish carrot and kasha squares,
    139
  Tuscan polenta loaf, 128
  see also bean
venison:
  currant and wheat bread loaf, 41
  and wild rice loaf, 40
vermicelli, sesame chicken squares
  with, 95
vitello tonnato loaf, 30

wheat bread, venison and currant loaf,
  41

yogurt-cucumber sauce, 155

zucchini:
  in chicken loaf tagine, 83
  in sausage ratatouille loaf, 26–27